R E I H E   C A N T Z

WOLFGANG WINTER
BERTHOLD HÖRBELT

herausgegeben von/*edited by* Florian Matzner

"The beverage case is a kind of 20th-century (and perhaps 21st-century) amphora. And if one abandons "time-honoured" materials such as stone, lard, etcetera—the traditional materials of sculpture—it seems to us that the plastic material "mineral-water case" is an entirely appropriate and perfectly adequate choice. We never developed a conceptual plan to work in this way, however. The process simply emerged in the studio and from our experiments." With this sober assessment, the artist duo of Wolfgang Winter and Berthold Hörbelt describe the development of their working approach over the past few years, a process that did indeed originate in the recognition of the aesthetic appeal of a random arrangement of beverage cases. First introduced to a broad international public at the exhibition "Skulptur. Projekte in Münster 1997", their beverage-case buildings have since embarked upon a tour through Germany, appearing at exhibitions in public space in Bonn, Berlin, Salzburg and Munich, and they will once again be able to demonstrate their substantial conceptual and aesthetic quality at the 48th Biennale d'Arte in Venice, to which the artists have been invited by Harald Szeemann. But Winter and Hörbelt have not confined themselves to creating scurrilous architectural sculptures out of stacked beverage cases. Projects of this kind are only one aspect of their co-operative relationship which began in 1992. Aside from the beverage-case buildings, their Same-Same projects in particular are certainly deserving of their first extensive publication in this small catalogue.

I wish to thank the co-authors Ammon Barzel (Berlin / Tel Aviv / Rome), Barbara Engelbach (Münster / Hamburg) and Wolfgang Ullrich (Munich) for their interest in the work of Winter and Hörbelt and their commitment to the realisation of this book project. Bernd Barde and Saskia H. Rothfischer of the Cantz publishing house have compiled and edited the substantial textual and photographic material in their typically reliable, painstaking and imaginative manner and put it into pleasing readable form.

Munich / Münster, April 1999

Florian Matzner

VORWORT

"Der Wasserkasten ist schließlich so etwas wie die Amphore des 20. Jahrhunderts, wahrscheinlich auch des 21. Jahrhunderts. Und wenn man sich von den 'gewachsenen' Materialien wie Stein, Fett etc, also den traditionellen Bildhauermaterialien, mal eben verabschiedet hat, ist das plastische Material 'Wasserkasten' in unseren Augen doch naheliegend und gerade gut genug. Es war jedoch nie konzeptuell angelegt, so zu arbeiten, sondern es wuchs quasi aus dem Atelier und den Experimenten heraus." Mit diesen nüchternen Worten beschreibt das Künstlerduo Wolfgang Winter und Berthold Hörbelt ihre Entwicklung der letzten Jahre, die ihren Anfang in der Tat im ästhetischen Reiz einer zufälligen Anhäufung von Wasserkästen genommen hat. Erstmals bei der Ausstellung *Skulptur. Projekte in Münster* 1997 einer breiten internationalen Öffentlichkeit bekannt geworden, sind die Kastenhäuser inzwischen mit Ausstellungen im Öffentlichen Raum in Bonn, Berlin, Salzburg und München durch ganz Deutschland gewandert und werden auf Einladung Harald Szeemanns bei der 48. Biennale d'Arte auch in Venedig einmal mehr mit ihrer konzeptuellen und ästhetischen Qualität überzeugen. – Aber Winter und Hörbelt stapeln nicht nur Wasserkästen zu skurrilen Architektur-Skulpturen aufeinander, diese sind nur ein Aspekt ihrer seit 1992 bestehenden Kooperation: Insbesondere auch die "Same-Same"-Projekte verdienen es neben den Kastenhäusern, erstmals durch dieses kleine Büchlein umfassend publiziert zu werden.
Ich danke den Co-Autoren Amnon Barzel (Berlin/Tel Aviv/Rom), Barbara Engelbach (Münster/Hamburg) und Wolfgang Ullrich (München) für ihr Interesse am Werk von Winter und Hörbelt und ihr Engagement bei der Entstehung des Buches.
Bernd Barde und Saskia H. Rothfischer aus dem Hause Cantz haben mit gewohnter Zuverlässigkeit, Präzision und Phantasie das umfangreiche Text- und Bildmaterial in eine lesefreundliche Form gebracht.

München/Münster, im April 1999   Florian Matzner

THE WORK OF WOLFGANG WINTER AND BERTHOLD HÖRBELT

A Fax Dialogue with Florian Matzner, January 1999

FLORIAN MATZNER (FM): *Seldom has a subject generated such controversy among European art theorists and critics in recent decades as the issue of what is commonly referred to as "art in public space". The inflation of "art in architecture" in Germany, a movement surely marked by good intentions but which tended to be more depressing than encouraging for artists and the public alike, was followed beginning in seventies by a tendency to abandon the sacred temple of the museum and take art into the streets. This did not include so-called "Drop Sculpture", works that appeared to have fallen from the skies as autonomous sculpture onto city streets and squares without any apparent reference to urban structure or to the history and psychology of the site at which they were located. No, the fashionable keyword was "site specificity": Artists were challenged to study the existing context throroughly and to place their works in a context of fruitful dialogue with the world of everyday life. The most important exhibition devoted to this theme was—and remains today—the Sculpture Projects in Münster, which took place for the third time in the small provincial capital of Münster in 1997. This exhibition, which despite its institutional character is still conceived as a laboratory experiment and a forum for discussion, was also the setting for your first major international success.*

You erected rather scurrilous structures at four different locations, "constructing" them from thousands of empty plastic mineral-water cases of the kind found in practically everyone's home—an everyday object that is as functionally indispensable as it is aesthetically superfluous. With these beverage cases you created mixed forms of architecture and sculpture that were used as information pavilions for the exhibition. There was considerable disagreement about the appearance of your works. Some people saw in them nothing but stacks of "beer cases" and responded with "I could do that, too!". Others contended that Marcel Duchamp's "pissoir" concept had finally been taken a step further, with earnestness, irony and a

ZUM WERK VON WOLFGANG WINTER UND BERTHOLD HÖRBELT

Ein Fax-Dialog mit Florian Matzner, Januar 1999

FLORIAN MATZNER (FM): Nur wenige Diskussionen in der europäischen und amerikanischen Kunsttheorie und Kunstkritik in den letzten Jahrzehnten sind so kontrovers geführt worden wie die um die sogenannte "Kunst im Öffentlichen Raum". Nach der Inflation der gutgemeinten "Kunst am Bau" in Deutschland, die eher deprimierend als ermutigend für die Künstler und das Publikum war, gab es seit den 70er Jahren die Tendenz, die heiligen Museumstempel zu verlassen und mit der Kunst auf die Straße zu gehen. Gemeint war hier aber nicht die "drop sculpture", die als autonome Skulptur wie vom Himmel auf städtische Plätze gefallen erschien, ohne jeden Bezug zur urbanen Struktur, zur Geschichte oder Psychologie ihres Aufstellungsortes. Vielmehr war die "site specificy" das Schlag- und Modewort: Künstler waren aufgefordert, sich intensiv mit dem vorgegebenen Kontext auseinanderzusetzen und ihre Werke in einen fruchtbaren Dialog mit der Alltagswelt zu setzen. Wichtigste Ausstellung zu diesem Thema sind nach wie vor die Skulptur-Projekte in Münster, die 1997 zum dritten Mal in der kleinen westfälischen Provinzhauptstadt Münster stattfanden. Diese Ausstellung, die sich trotz ihrer Institutionalisierung weiterhin als Laborversuch, als Diskussionsforum versteht, markiert gleichzeitig Euren ersten großen internationalen Erfolg.

An vier stadtplanerisch prominenten Stellen hattet Ihr skurrile Gebilde aufge-

sense of both the genial and the banal, in a pioneering advance toward the future after 100 years of standstill in art.

WOLFGANG WINTER (WW): *During the last two years we have done several beverage-case projects. Still, it is always a new and exciting experience to see how things we have planned in advance actually turn out in practice. The fact that they—the beverage-case houses—cause controversy is not a bad thing, as long as the discussion remains objective and doesn't go below the belt—something we've experienced as well. To a certain extent it's in the nature of things, since our structures are really not that useful as purely functional buildings. There is no way for us to hide under the cloak of utilitarian service. Instead, we try to find an occasion for our rather bulky things, because we do live and take part in the world, after all. Nevertheless, there is a big difference between erecting a sculpture that is clearly defined as autonomous, on the one hand, and putting up a large-scale sculpture that can be walked through, a work that represents a provocation by virtue of its material character and elicits commensurate responses. The issue has nothing to do with a rejection of autonomous art, however. It has to do with creating an interface between autonomy and utility. Working that out is the objective of our beverage-case projects.*

What really makes the beverage-case installations vulnerable, I think, is not their material character itself but the fact that they can be walked through, meaning that they can be used by anyone at any given time. That can be very positive for us, when someone discovers the wonderful transparency of the beverage cases and the visual qualities of the beverage-case house in general, for example; but it can also lead to a scandal—as it did in Salzburg in 1998, when even the local suffragan bishop felt called upon to make a very reactionary statement. People like that feel provoked automatically by anything that is new, and without even honouring it with a glance they burst into an outcry, denying the "so-called" artists any competence whatsoever. In comparison, comments like "I could do that, too!" are harmless. To the credit of our clients at the time, we have to say that they consistently defended the sculpture and allowed it to remain standing at Salzburg's "Alter Markt" until the exhibition was over. They did not give in to the pressure exerted by Salzburg conservatives. What is more, the issue of sculpture in public space has been a subject of

stellt, "gebaut" aus tausenden Wasserkästen, wie sie jedermann zu Hause stehen hat, ein Alltagsgegenstand, der funktional ebenso unabdingbar wie ästhetisch überflüssig ist. Aus diesen Wasserkästen hattet Ihr Mischformen aus Architektur und Skulptur errichtet, die als Informationspavillons für die Ausstellung genutzt wurden und an deren Erscheinungsformen sich die Geister des Publikums teilten: die einen sprachen ständig von "Bierkästen" und meinten "Das kann ich auch!", die anderen behaupteten, endlich sei das Konzept des "Pissoir" von Marcel Duchamp nach beinahe 100 Jahren Stillstand in der Kunst mit Ernst und Ironie, mit Sinn für das Geniale und das Banale zukunftsweisend weiterentwickelt worden.

WOLFGANG WINTER (WW): Wir haben in den letzten beiden Jahren nun schon einige Kastenhaus-Projekte gemacht; es ist trotzdem immer wieder neu und aufregend, zu erleben wie die vorher geplanten Dinge sich in der Praxis dann bewähren. Daß sie – die Kastenhäuser – kontrovers diskutiert werden, ist nicht schlecht, so lange die Diskussion sachlich bleibt und nicht unter die Gürtellinie geht, was wir natürlich auch schon erlebt haben. Gewissermaßen bleibt das ja auch in der Natur der Sache, denn so nützlich als reine Zweckgebäude sind unsere Gebilde ja nicht, so daß man sich also nicht unter dem Deckmantel der Dienlichkeit verstecken könnte. Vielmehr stellen wir unseren eher sperrigen Dingen gerne einen Anlaß voran, auch weil wir ja in der Welt leben und teilnehmen.

Es ist trotzdem ein großer Unterschied, ob nun eine klar als autonom definierte Skulptur aufgestellt wird, oder wir andererseits eine begehbare Großskulptur plazieren, die schon allein durch ihre Materialität bedingt eine Provokation darstellt und dementsprechend rezipiert wird. Bei all dem muß klar sein, daß es nicht um eine Ablehung von autonomer Skulptur geht, sondern um die Schnittstelle zwischen Autonomie und Anwendbarkeit; diese herauszuarbeiten ist Thema der Kastenhaus-Projekte.

Kastenhaus 576.9, 1998, Salzburg, Alter Markt

Die eigentliche Verletzlichkeit der Kastenhäuser liegt meiner Meinung nach aber nicht in ihrer Materialität, sondern in der Tatsache, daß sie begehbar sind, also von jedermann zu jeder Zeit irgendwie zu gebrauchen sind. Das kann einer-

discussion in Salzburg since then, and that was not the case before the exhibition. Ultimately—and this is what makes our work so exciting—only our own criticism counts. In other words, we are the ones who decide about the quality of a sculpture, and the first sketches, the very first preliminary steps determine how good the thing will be when it is finished.

BERTHOLD HÖRBELT (BH): *Rejection and responses like "I could do that, too!" will always be part of the picture—but in the case of our beverage-case installation there were many visitors, including people who knew nothing about art history, who were astonished by the aesthetic quality achieved by stacking the mineral-water cases and by the transparency of the spaces created in this way. Of course we were truly surprised by the extremely negative attitude of the punkers who hung around the area during the daytime towards our beverage-case installation in Münster's Salzstraße. We had restricted and accelerated the flow of visitors with our Bauzaun (Construction Fence), which made it harder for the punkers to do their panhandling. Later they explained to us that the ideal targets for panhandling were people strolling aimlessly across the square.*

FM: *You've mentioned several important aspects that I think make the "long-term experiment" with the beverage-case houses you have conducted since 1096 in Schwarzach, Münster, Salzburg, Berlin and most recently in Bonn synonymous with the opportunities and possibilities open to "art today": One of these is the use of so-called everyday materials, in this case the mineral-water cases that were borro-*

Kastenhaus 1330.11, 1998, Bonn, Kunst- und Ausstellungshalle der Bundesrepublik Deutschland

seits erfreulich für uns sein, wenn zum Beispiel jemand die wunderbare Transparenz der Kästen und überhaupt die visuellen Qualitäten des Kastenhauses entdeckt; das kann aber auch – wie 1998 in Salzburg – zu einem Skandal führen, der selbst den ortsansässigen Weihbischof zu sehr reaktionärem Wort bemüßigte. Solche Leute fühlen sich per se von allem Neuen provoziert und ohne überhaupt nur hinzusehen, geben sie einen Aufschrei von sich und streiten den "sogenannten" Künstlern jegliche Kompetenz ab. Dann sind Kommentare wie "Das kann ich auch!" noch harmlos. Unseren damaligen Auftraggebern muß man jedenfalls zugute halten, daß sie die Skulptur stets verteidigten und bis zum Ende der Ausstellung auf Salzburgs "Altem Markt" beließen, also dem Druck der konservativen Salzburger nicht wichen; überdies wird seitdem in Salzburg über moderne Skulptur im öffentlichen Raum grundsätzlicher diskutiert, was vorher nicht so der Fall war.

Letztlich – und das macht diese Arbeit so aufregend – zählt doch nur die eigene Kritik, also der, der letztlich über die Qualität einer Skulptur entscheidet, ist man selber, und mit der ersten Entwurfsskizze, mit dem Anfangen, mit der allerersten Überlegung entscheidet sich schon, wie gut das Ding später einmal sein wird.

BERTHOLD HÖRBELT (BH): Ablehnung und Meinungen wie "Das kann ich auch!" wird man immer finden – bei unseren Kastenhäusern waren jedoch viele Besucher, auch diejenigen ohne kunsthistorische Kenntnisse verblüfft über die durch ihre Stapelung gewonnene ästhetische Qualität der Wasserkästen und über die Transparenz der so geschaffenen Räume. Überrascht hat uns allerdings wirklich die äußerst ablehnende Haltung der sich hier tagsüber aufhaltenden Punker gegenüber unserem Kastenhaus auf der Salzstraße in Münster. Wir hatten durch unseren "Bauzaun" den Fußgängerstrom eingeengt und somit beschleunigt, wodurch das Schnorren für die Punker schwieriger wurde. Später erklärten sie uns, der ideale Kunde fürs Anschnorren wäre derjenige, der ziel- und richtungslos über einen Platz geht.

FM: Ihr habt einige wichtige Aspekte angesprochen, die Euren "Langzeitversuch" mit den Kastenhäusern seit 1996 in Schwarzach, Münster, Salzburg, Berlin und zuletzt in Bonn für mich zu einem Synonym für die Chancen und Möglichkeiten von "Kunst heute" machen: Zum einen die Verwendung von sogenannten Alltagsmaterialien, hier die Wasserkästen, die für die Laufzeit einer Kunstausstellung aus

wed from the industrial circulation system of "buying—bringing home—emptying—returning—repurchasing" for the duration of an art exhibition, objects which, because of their material composition, their function and their visual appearance do not belong to the "realm of art" per se but instead to the sphere of dull everyday routine. You transform these objects—the beverage cases—into architectural sculptures, imbuing them with an astonishing aesthetic quality before they return again at the end of the exhibition to the industrial circulation process—a different, better kind of recycling!

Another important aspect is that your works can indeed be used. They have a concrete function apart from the dull everyday routine mentioned above. They serve as movie theatres, as bus stops or as information pavilions. Thus the viewer / visitor / user is assigned an active role, which he or she is happy to play. In this way, the beverage-case installations become "services" and Winter and Hörbelt become "public-service artists".

Last but not least, I myself was fascinated—when I first met you—by your first beverage-case installation for the rehabilitation centre in Schwarzach, which was planned as part of a play and theme garden. During the realization phase I had the opportunity to help sick and disabled people as they became active participants and influential factors in the project for which you provided the "framework"—the beverage-case installation—while the rehabilitation center patients took charge of the "decorations". Thus your work as artists was subject to a certain degree of risk, as the "interventions" of the patients could not be planned or controlled.

In summary, what fascinates both your positive and negative critics alike—in my opinion—is that fact that a mundane object such as a mineral-water case can develop so many aesthetic and functional qualities. Or, to put it differently: After being transformed into an "object of aesthetic desire", the "new" utility value of the beverage case is several times greater than its "old" real value.

BH: You mention durations and the industrial circulation system involving the beverage cases. It is in this context that we see the chance for our temporary beverage-case installations within the discussion about "art in public space" at this time. We are interested in the kind of spatial change that takes place within the city over a limited period of time. The square in front of the Karstadt department store pres-

Aufbau Kastenhaus 1330.11, 1998
Bonn, Kunst- und Ausstellungshalle der
Bundesrepublik Deutschland

dem Industriekreislauf von "Kaufen – Nachhause-bringen – Leertrinken – Zurückbringen – Neukaufen" entliehen werden, Gegenstände also, die auf Grund ihres Materials, ihrer Funktion und ihrer visuellen Erscheinung per se nicht dem "Kunstbereich" zuge-ordnet sind, sondern der alltäglichen stupiden Bewältigung des Alltags dienen. Diese Objekte – die Wasserkästen – werden von Euch in Architektur-Skulpturen transformiert, haben unvermittelt eine überraschende ästhetische Qualität und kehren nach Ende der Ausstellung unversehrt in den Industriekreislauf zurück – eine andere, bessere Art des Recycling!

Zum zweiten sind Eure Arbeiten in der Tat benutzbar, sie haben eine konkre-te Funktion neben der genannten stupiden Bewältigung des Alltags: sie fungieren als Kino, als Bushaltestelle oder als Informationspavillon. Dem Betrachter/Besu-cher/Benutzer wird damit eine aktive Rolle zugewiesen, die er gerne spielt. Die Kastenhäuser werden damit zu "Dienstleistungen", Winter und Hörbelt zu "Künst-lern im Öffentlichen Dienst".

Last not least hat mich persönlich – als ich Euch kennengelernt habe – Euer erstes Kastenhaus für das Rehabilitationszentrum in Schwarzach fasziniert, das als Teil eines Spiel- und Erfahrungsgartens geplant worden ist. Bei der Reali-sierung haben kranke und behinderte Menschen geholfen, sie wurden damit zu einem aktiven Bestandteil und Faktor des Projektes, bei dem Ihr den "Rahmen" – das Kastenhaus – vorgegeben habt, während die Patienten des Rehabilitations-zentrums für die "Dekoration" verantwortlich waren. Eure künstlerische Arbeit war damit einem gewissen "Risikofaktor" ausgesetzt, waren die "Eingriffe" der Patien-ten doch nicht plan- und beeinflußbar.

Zusammenfassend fasziniert – so glaube ich – sowohl die positiven wie nega-tiven Kritiker Eurer Arbeit, daß ein banaler Wasserkasten als Kunstgegenstand so viele ästhetische und funktionale Qualitäten entwickeln kann – oder anders formu-liert: nach seiner Transformation in ein "Objekt künstlerischer Begierde" hat sich der "neue" Gebrauchswert des Wasserkastens gegenüber seinem "alten" Real-wert um einiges vervielfacht.

BH: Du sprichst oben von Laufzeiten und vom Industriekreislauf der Wasser-

ented an entirely different "face" during the Sculpture Project in Münster, for example. And we experienced the public's responses—which ranges from "tear it down"
in Salzburg to "let it stand" in Bonn.

The "Lichtspielhau" (Movie Theatre) for the "Künstlerhaus Bethanien" in
Berlin is another story. It was planned as a cinema (and approved by the authori-
ties). And in the case of our beverage-case installation for the rehabilitation center
our work even included planning for the gardens. With respect to these projects I
would tend to speak of concrete commissions rather than "services".

WW: The beverage case is a kind of 20th-century (and perhaps 21st-century)
amphora. And if one abandons "time-honoured" materials such as stone, lard,
etcetera—the traditional materials of sculpture—it seems to us that the plastic
material "mineral-water case" is an entirely appropriate and perfectly adequate choice. We never developed a conceptual plan to work in this way, however. The process simply emerged in the studio and from our experiments. In 1995 we developed a type of plastic we called HOEWI 301, a protein-based mass we used for a
series of highly reduced molded sculptures. It closely resembled the beverage case
in terms of its material aesthetics. Thus it became logical at some point to spare
ourselves the effort of producing this material and to make direct use of the plastic
cases as workable modelling material. This phase of our work was ultimately very
laboratory-oriented. We wanted to prepare suitable experiments for all of our theo-
retical explorations in sculpture.

FM: Which brings us to another important aspect of your work, one that is overs-
hadowed to a certain extent by the major beverage-case-installation projects that
have earned you international acclaim in recent years. In this regard I would be
interested to know whether anyone outside of Germany has "ordered" a sculpture
comprised of beverage cases from you. The reason I ask is that in the case of a
beverage-case installation—stacked in France or Italy, in England, Sweden, the US
or Japan—the basic unit of the mineral-water case would probably not be identified
per se as a plain everyday object but as an aesthetically unconventional cast form
created by equally unconventional artists.

BH: In our beverage-case-installation project in Salzburg we were already operating
in a foreign country, so to speak (the case-circulation system functions only in the

kästen. Darin liegt wahrscheinlich derzeitig die Chance unserer temporären innerhalb der Diskussion "Kunst im öffentlichen Raum". Uns interessiert die zeitlich begrenzte, räumliche Veränderung innerhalb einer Stadt. So hatte z. B. der Platz vor Karstadt während der Skulptur-Projekte in Münster ein völlig anderes "Gesicht". Weiter hatten wir ja auch Publikumsreaktionen, von "Abräumen" in Salzburg bis "Stehenlassen" in Bonn.

Anders verhält es sich mit dem "Lichtspielhaus" für das "Künstlerhaus Bethanien" in Berlin. Es wurde als Kino geplant (und behördlich abgenommen). Und bei unserem Kastenhaus für das Rehabilitationszentrum reichte unsere Arbeit bis in die Planungen der Gartenanlage hinein. Bei diesen Projekten würde ich nicht von "Dienstleistungen", sondern von konkretem Auftrag sprechen.

WW: Der Wasserkasten ist schließlich so etwas wie die Amphore des 20. Jahrhunderts, wahrscheinlich auch des 21. Jahrhunderts. Und wenn man sich von den "gewachsenen" Materialien wie Stein, Fett etc., also den traditionellen Bildhauermaterialien, mal eben verabschiedet, ist das plastische Material "Wasserkasten" in unseren Augen doch sehr naheliegend und gerade gut genug. Es war jedoch nie konzeptuell angelegt, so zu arbeiten, sondern es wuchs quasi aus dem Atelier und den Experimenten heraus. Wir entwickelten 1995 eine Art Kunststoff, welchen wir HOEWI 301 nannten, eine auf Proteinen basierende Masse, die wir für eine Serie von sehr reduziert geformten Skulpturen verwendeten, und deren Materialästhetik den Wasserkästen sehr nahe kam. Während wir den Getränketransportkasten in seiner Funktion als "Verkehrswesen" entdecken, verfolgen die HOEWI-Materialanalysen die Nahrungsmittelwege und die Resteverwertung bis hin zu den Abdeckereien; Dort werden die unverzehrten Reste von Tierkörpern, also Häute, Innereien und Knochen, zu Tierleim verarbeitet, welcher die Grundsubstanz der HOEWI-Blöcke bildet. Jene sind deshalb über ihre Erscheinung als abstrakte Skulptur hinaus ein Beitrag zum bildnerischen Thema Tierdarstellung. Letztlich hatte diese Phase unserer Arbeit einen enormen Laborcharakter. Wir wollten eigentlich zu allen unseren skulptur-theoretischen Fragestellungen die passenden Experimente bereitstellen.

FM: Wir kommen damit zu einem anderen wichtigen Aspekt Eurer Arbeit, der gewissermaßen im Schatten der großen Kastenhaus-Projekte steht, die Euch in

FRG). The response in Salzburg was "Jetzt stellt's auch noch Euere Deitschen Kasten daher . . ." (So now you're even bringing in your German cases . . .). But on the other hand, a beverage case of this kind can be readily identified as an industrially manufactured product just about anywhere.

FM: *As mentioned already, the other important, although less well-known aspect of your artistic co-operation involves autonomous sculptures (and sculpture groups) that are also developed into large-scale spatial installations. I am thinking of the Madonna figure, for example, the original model (from the 1950s) for which was reproduced in numerous castings and—thanks to the material HOEWI 301—a number of radically altered "copies". What does this material actually consist of?*

BH: *From a so-called prototype, in this case a 1950s Madonna borrowed from a church, we take a skin made of soft rubber, which in turn is cast (after being partially turned inside out), in a process in which the flow of the material, among other things, determines the form. We also added the arm of a crucified Christ to the "Madonna". We welcome any random effects that emerge in the process and contribute to shaping the appearance of the sculpture. In concrete terms, what remains is not the replica of a newly created Madonna but its content, which is expressed in the title of the prototype.*

In contrast to the "same-same" process, no prototype preceeds our work with HOEWI 301 (the material is composed from animal components). The objects cast in molds or frames change as the material dries and gradually hardens.

FM: *You describe these pieces, on which you have worked together since 1992, as products of a "same-same process", a term that is somewhat difficult to translate into German. This idea of like images doesn't quite accord with reality, however, since the Madonna statue from the 1950s, like the neo-classical bust of Voltaire, is altered through by the casting process and the changes in material that take place during the six months or more of drying. In other words, the work develops its "own" final form. What strikes me as important about this process is that it nullifies all aspects of serial production, since every casting is undeniably a one-of-a-kind piece. On the other hand, the "independent character" of the material gives the works a certain element of randomness that is beyond your own influence.*

WW: *To return to your earlier question regarding sculptures in public space—there*

den letzten beiden Jahren international bekannt gemacht haben. In diesem Zusammenhang würde mich aber noch interessieren, ob schon jemand außerhalb von Deutschland bei Euch eine Arbeit aus Wasserkästen "bestellt" hat, denn bei einem Kastenhaus – aufgestapelt in Frankreich oder Italien, in England oder Schweden, in den USA oder in Japan – würde die Kleinform des Wasserkastens vermutlich nicht per se als banale Alltagsform identifiziert werden können, sondern als eine ästhetisch eigenwillige Gußform ebenso eigenwilliger Künstler?

BH: Bei unserem Kastenhaus für Salzburg bewegten wir uns – der Kreislauf dieser Kästen funktioniert nur in der BRD – sozusagen bereits im Ausland. O-Ton: "Jetzt stellt's auch noch Euere Deitschen Kasten daher..." Andererseits kann so ein Wasserkasten überall als industriell gefertigtes Massenprodukt identifiziert werden.

FM: Wie gesagt, der andere wichtige, aber eher unbekannte Aspekt Eurer künstlerischen Kooperation sind autonome Skulpturen(-Gruppen), die gegebenenfalls zu großen Rauminstallationen entwickelt werden. Ich denke zum Beispiel an die Madonnen-Figur, deren Original aus den 50er Jahren in zahlreichen Abgüssen und – begründet durch das Material HOEWI 301 – in teilweise extrem verfremdeten "Kopien" vervielfältigt wurde. Woraus genau besteht dieses Material?

BH: Von einem sogenannten Prototyp, hier bei einer aus der Kirche entliehenen 50er-Jahre-Madonna, wird eine Haut aus weichem Kautschuk abgenommen, die wiederum (teilweise umgestülpt) ausgegossen wird, wobei unter anderem der Fluß des Materials die Form bestimmt. Zusätzlich fügten wir der "Madonna" den Arm eines gekreuzigten Jesus an. Dabei auftretende Zufälle kommen uns gerade recht für das so entstandene Erscheinungsbild der Skulptur: konkret bleibt eigentlich nicht das Abbild einer neu geschaffenen Madonna, sondern deren Inhalt. Der findet sich im Titel des Prototyps wieder.

Anders als beim "Same-Same-Prozeß" geht bei den Arbeiten mit

Kastenhaus 90.5 (Bus Stop), 1998, Havixbeck

are the Drop Sculptures, which represent a very dubious artistic practice and only very rarely do justice to the criteria for art in public spaces. At best, such sculptures serve as unrelated decorative additions that do nothing for the identity and the profile of their surroundings.

If we look closely at a modern big city with all of the dynamic processes in encompasses, it becomes clear that the location-oriented composition of a work of art or, in other words, a work adapted specifically to existing spatial, social or historical aspects, conceived as a counter-model to Drop Sculptures (which surfaced as the essence of the Sculpture Projects in 1987) is difficult to realize in the real world. I have a clear recollection of Remy Zaugg's article in the 1987 Münster sculpture catalogue, in which he formulated a wonderful, idealized description of the tasks facing an artist working in public space. Yet we must remember that it is the rapidly changing spatial situation in a big city that makes such an approach so difficult. No one can guarantee that a high-rise building or a bridge will not have to be erected next to the sculpture a year later, casting the sculpture in shadows the whole day through and negating all of the artist's efforts to achieve social relationships, to give concrete expression to historical aspects, proportions and axes of view until there is virtually nothing left of the space-creating, identity-building power of a publicly exhibited work of art. It is a plain and simple fact that a total shift in our approach to sculpture is necessary if sculpture is to retain at least its presence in public space. At the moment it appears as if this flux that affects society as a whole and planning processes has to be taken into account as well. But that also means that public places as familiar settings of communal life as they "there once were" will cease to exist. They are relatively unimportant. Vision, the act of seeing, is no longer static and focused; instead, the perception of visual impressions proceeds more from the corners of the eyes, from motion. Locale will be replaced by routes of travel. We accompany each other a part of the way, communicating as we move, and then go our separate ways. A banal example of this is a train trip that is more familiar to some people than the corner pub, a place which is designed for communication—a trip that takes place at high speed but, strangely enough, in perfect serenity and is limited in time by the point arrival at a destination. Our beverage-case installation in Bonn and our Bauzaun in Münster called

HOEWI 301 (das Material ist auf der Basis von Tierelementen aufgebaut) kein Prototyp voraus. Die in Formen oder Rahmen gegossenen Objekte verändern sich durch Austrocknen und langsames Aushärten des Materials.

FM: Ihr beschreibt diese Arbeiten, die in Kooperation seit 1992 entstehen, als "Same-Same-Prozeß", das heißt im deutschen etwas schwer zu übersetzen als "Gleiches vom Gleichen": Dies entspricht natürlich nicht der Realität, denn ein Madonnen-Statue aus den 50er Jahren ebenso wie eine klassizistische Portrait-Büste von Voltaire werden durch das Abgußverfahren und die dem Material und seinem langen, teilweise mehr als sechsmonatigem Vorgang des Trocknens sich selbst überlassen, das heißt das Werk bildet seine "eigene" endgültige Form aus. Wichtig für mich ist an diesem Prozeß, daß zum einen jedwede Art der seriellen Produktion unterlaufen wird, denn jeder Abguß ist unbestritten ein Unikat, auf der anderen Seite aber ist auf Grund der "Eigenwilligkeit" des Materials den Arbeiten ein gewisser Zufallsfaktor zu eigen, auf den Ihr keinen Einfluß mehr habt.

WW: Was Deine vorhergehende Frage betreffs Skulpturen im öffentlichen Raum betrifft: Da sind zum einen die Drop Sculptures, die ja doch sehr zweifelhaft sind als künstlerische Praxis und den Ansprüchen einer Kunst für den öffentlichen Raum nur in seltenen Fällen gerecht werden. Die Skulptur wird dann bestenfalls zum beziehungslosen dekorativen Beiwerk, bringt aber nichts für die Identität und Konturierung des sie umgebenden Ortes, der Gegend.

Sieht man jetzt aber eine moderne Großstadt mit all ihrer Dynamik, so wird deutlich, daß eine ortsbezogene Konfektion eines Kunstwerkes, also ein Zuschnitt auf spezifische räumliche, soziale oder historisch relevante Momente als Gegen-modell der Drop Sculptures (1987 als Essenz der Skulpturenprojekte aufschei-nend) in der Realität schwierig zu verwirklichen ist. Ich erinnere mich sehr gut an Remy Zaugg's Text im Skulptur-Katalog Münster 1987, wo er in wunderbarer Weise das Aufgabenfeld eines für den öffentlichen Raum arbeitenden Künstlers sehr ide-alisierend formuliert. Aber: Zum einen ist es die sich rapide verändernde räum-liche Situation innerhalb einer Großstadt, die eine solche Vorgehensweise er-schwert. Keiner kann garantieren, daß nicht im nächsten Jahr neben der Skulptur ein Hochhaus oder eine Brücke gebaut werden muß, die dann den ganzen Tag die Skulptur im Schatten stehen läßt, sämtliche Bemühungen des Künstlers um so-

attention to this theme. They were works in which sculpture is not understood as something static and does not call upon the viewer to "stand still and observe the sculpture" or to "go in, stay inside a while and feel the space". Instead, it says: "You are in motion. Go through here, and you can experience—by the way—what it is like to walk through a pass made of beverage cases. (You can even see it out of the corners of your eyes as you walk. [. . .]"

Although this does encourage a form of consumption, it also provides a contemporary interface with a "slow" medium such as sculpture once was. That, at least, is one of the important aspects that distinguishes a beverage-case installation like that in Bonn from the one in, say, Berlin.

FM: *It is certainly true that modes of perception—and the visual sense is the most important of sense available to human beings—have undergone fundamental change in the course of the last few years and decades. This can be attributed to the influence of new visual media: TV in the early post-war years of the fifties, the computer since the seventies and the Internet, e-mail and electronic superhighways that have reduced global events to the supposedly manageable dimensions of a mediaeval town square since the early nineties. All of this will surely lead us into a phase of transition from the industrial society we have cultivated for several centuries to a new form commonly referred to as the Information Society. Yet I still believe—and this is where our views diverge—that the urban context of a city will gain in importance as a setting and stage for human communal life for the very reasons you describe, and it will survive and retain its viability, because we still know the answer to the question "Is virtual sex more important than real sex?"*

Kastenhaus 2640.15 (Lichtspielhaus), 1998
Berlin, Künstlerhaus Bethanien, The Cinema Project

It seems to me that the rapid pace of reception today is vehemently opposed by the desire for stasis, for slowness, for real experiences. This is at least one of the

ziale Bezüge, Konkretisierung historischer Momente, Proportionen, Blickachsen und dergleichen zunichte gemacht sind, bis dann von der raumschaffenden, identitätsstiftenden Kraft eines öffentlich ausgestellten Kunstwerkes nichts mehr zu spüren ist. Es ist schlichtweg so, daß sich der Ansatz von Skulptur komplett verschieben muß, um zumindest im öffentlichen urbanen Raum präsent sein zu können. Derzeit sieht es so aus, daß man dieses Fließen im Verhalten der ganzen Gesellschaft und in ihrem Planen mit berücksichtigen muß; das heißt aber auch, daß es öffentliche Orte als vertraute Stätten des Zusammenlebens nicht in dem Maße geben wird, wie das 'mal war: Sie sind relativ unwichtig. Auch der Blick, das Sehen ist nicht mehr statisch und zentriert, sondern die Wahrnehmung visueller Eindrücke erfolgt mehr aus den Augenwinkeln, aus der Bewegung heraus. Die Örtlichkeit wird ersetzt durch den Weg, wir begleiten uns ein Stück, tauschen uns aus und gehen auseinander. Banales Beispiel ist eine Zugreise, der manchem schon vertrauter ist als die Eckkneipe, ein Ort, der auf Kommunikation angelegt ist – eine Reise, die komischerweise in hoher Geschwindigkeit seelenruhig stattfindet und zeitlich begrenzt ist durch das Ankaommen am Zielort. Unser Bonner Kastenhaus oder unsere "Bauzaun"-Arbeit in Münster waren Arbeiten, die dies thematisieren, also die Skulptur nicht als etwas Statisches begreifen, vom Betrachter nicht fordern: "Bleib stehen und betrachte die Skulptur als Gegenüber", auch nicht "Geh hinein, bleib einen Augenblick drinnen und fühle den Raum", sondern: "Du bist in Bewegung, geh hier durch, und dann kannst Du – by the way – erfahren, wie es ist, wenn man durch einen Paß aus Getränkekisten geht. (Du kannst es sogar aus den Augenwinkeln im Laufen sehen...)"

Hier ist dann zwar schon eine Form des Konsumierens provoziert, aber es stellt auch eine zeitgemäße Schnittstelle eines "langsamen" Mediums, wie es Skulptur ehemals war, bereit. Das ist auch zumindest ein wichtiger Aspekt, der ein Kastenhaus wie das in Bonn von dem z.B. in Berlin unterscheidet.

FM: Es ist zwar richtig, daß sich in den letzten Jahren und Jahrzehnten die Art der Wahrnehmung – und die optische oder visuelle ist die wichtigste unter den, dem Menschen zur Verfügung stehenden Sinnen – grundsätzlich verändert hat. Dies ist sicherlich auf die neuen Bildmedien zurückzuführen: nach dem Krieg in den 50er Jahren der Fernseher, seit den 70er Jahren der Computer und seit den frühen 90er

reasons why we recognize a growing new interest on the part of both artists and the public in the relationship between architecture and nature and between art and the landscape in recent years. And that it why I am convinced that we need an alternative to this fleeting "perception from the corners of one's eyes'—as you refer to it—namely the slow "concentration on the center of focus".

Of course your beverage-case installations, like the one in front of the Bundeskunsthalle in Bonn or outside the Karstadt department store in Münster, are "walk-by pieces", sculptures seen by viewers out of the corners of their eyes as they hurry past them. Yet this is precisely the opportunity offered by contemporary art in public urban space: to stop briefly, to focus on what one sees, to enter "a different world" for a moment, to escape if only for that one moment the daily cycle of "sleeping-working-eating-sleeping" and to find a visual, tactile and psychological alternative in art. This is what has always fascinated me most about your beverage-case installations: the transformation of one of the most mundane objects of our everyday world into a visible, alternative "counterworld" that truly offers the viewer/visitor / passer-by this kind of visual, tactile and psychological freedom.

WW: Well, just to make sure that we understand one another correctly: What I am committed to is the interplay of the arts and architecture within the urban environment. I would go so far as to say that true urbanity is possible only when art is present in urban space. I wish we could have in our cities the same lightness and even cheerfulness, if you will, that we find much more of elsewhere. And by the same token I would wish to have places of remembrance such as cemeteries or certain memorials can be, for example. But I also think that real places that bring people together, like the large old squares with their central, dominant sculptures, cannot grow forth as the products of some romantic longing but must instead respond to modern needs and modes of perception.

And that is why our beverage-case projects make me feel more like a street musician who sets up on some streetcorner and hopes that his songs are good enough to keep him from being chased away.

To return to our sculpture Bauzaun, the project we developed for the Sculpture Projects in downtown Münster: We were not at all happy with the way this site, this left-over spot in the heart of the city presented itself. A really quite unpleasant work

Jahren Internet, e-mail und Electronic Superhighways, die das Weltgeschehen auf die vermeintliche Überschaubarkeit eines mittelalterlichen Dorfplatzes reduzieren. All dies wird in der Tat zum Übergang von der seit mehreren hundert Jahren verbindlichen Industriegesellschaft zu einer neuen Form führen, die man mit dem Begriff der Informationsgesellschaft zu umschreiben sucht. Trotzdem glaube ich – und da bin ich mit Dir nicht einer Meinung – , daß der urbane Kontext einer Stadt als Rahmen und Bühne menschlichen Zusammenlebens gerade deshalb immer mehr an Bedeutung gewinnt und sich bewähren muß, denn die Frage "Ist Virtual Sex wichtiger als Real Sex?" kann immer noch eindeutig beantwortet werden.

Der Schnelligkeit heutiger Rezeption steht meines Erachtens der Wunsch nach Statik, nach Langsamkeit, nach realen Erlebnissen vehement gegenüber. Nicht zuletzt deshalb kann man in der Kunst der letzten Jahre eine neue Vorliebe der Künstler und des Publikums für das Verhältnis von Architektur und Natur, von Kunst und Landschaft konstatieren. Ich glaube deshalb, daß der schnellen "Wahrnehmung aus den Augenwinkeln" – wie Du es nennst – die langsame "Focussierung im Blickpunkt" entgegengesetzt werden muß.

Natürlich sind Eure Kastenhäuser wie etwa das in Bonn vor der Bundeskunsthalle oder in Münster vor dem Karstadt-Kaufhaus "Laufarbeiten", die der Betrachter als Passant im Vorübereilen "aus den Augenwinkeln" zur Kenntnis nimmt. Andererseits ist dies aber doch genau die Chance zeitgenössischer Kunst im öffentlichen Stadtraum: kurz anzuhalten, sich zu konzentrieren auf das, was man sieht, kurz in eine "andere Welt" einzutauchen, dem täglichen Kreislauf aus "Schlafen-Arbeiten-Essen-Schlafen" zumindest für einen Augenblick zu entfliehen, und in der Kunst eine visuelle, haptische und psychologische Alternative zu sehen. Genau dies hat mich an Euren Kastenhäusern immer fasziniert: die Transformation eines der banalsten Gegenstände unseres Alltags in eine sichtbar alternative "Gegenwelt", die dem Betrachter/Besucher/Passant eben in der Tat diese visuelle, haptische und psychologische Freiheit anbietet.

ww: Also, daß wir uns hier nicht falsch verstehen: Wofür ich einstehen möchte, ist das Zusammenspiel der Künste, der Architektur innerhalb des städtischen Raumes; ich glaube sogar, daß eine wirkliche Urbanität erst dann zu spüren ist, wenn

Entwurfzeichnung zu Skulptur. Projekte in Münster, 1997
Mischtechnik auf Papier; 60 x 84 cm

of art was erected there in a very complicated installation (I mean those flags) in order to keep the emptiness from being noticed. A department store facade with racy spoilers and a new department store building were erected opposite an old church. The spatial or architectural aspects addressed by the new structures are impossible to make out. Of course they also grouped benches around the trees—those prefab things—and put in historical-looking paving stones—a typical German pedestrian zone, in other words, and a missed opportunity on top of that.

We wanted our beverage-case construction fence to offer a way of crossing the square without becoming a part of this dubious ensemble, to "beam" people across the square, so to speak. To all of the worlds gathered together here we deliberately added yet another so that somehow nothing fit together at all. The tragic part of the story is that it may not have been clear enough what we were really trying to do. Some people thought that the "colorful ensemble of sheetmetal flags" through which our beverage-case installation wound its way was part of our work of art, as if we had built those things ourselves as decoration for our beverage-case architecture. I think this kind of intervention was articulated with greater clarity in front of the Bundeskunsthalle, and the irony was more obvious.

Whether it bothers us when Japanese viewers, for example, interpret our beverage cases as original forms cast by the artists' hands rather than returnable bottle racks used by the beverage trade? Let me use the image of the musician again: We play our instrument as if we had invented it. And we play our own compositions on it. I wouldn't dream of asking a person from India whether he had invented his sitar himself, just because it doesn't look like a guitar. [. . .] What is more, every material, and this includes our beverage cases, is but a tool, perhaps one with a very special life of its own but mute nonetheless, because it constantly seeks to remind us of our earthly existence through their presence.

Kunst sich im städtischen Raum thematisiert. Ich hätte in unseren Städten gerne diese Leichtigkeit und meinetwegen auch Heiterkeit, wie sie anderswo mehr zu spüren ist. Genauso wünsche ich mir Orte des Erinnerns, wie es beispielsweise Friedhöfe sein können, oder manche Denkmäler es sein können. Aber ich glaube auch, daß die Entstehung von tatsächlichen Orten, die die Menschen zusammenführen, wie es ehemals die großen Plätze mit ihren zentralen platzbestimmenden Skulpturen waren, nicht aus einer romantisierenden Sehnsucht heraus passieren kann, sondern echten modernen Bedürfnissen und Wahrnehmungsweisen Folge leisten muß.

Deshalb fühle ich mich mit unseren Kastenhaus-Projekten derzeit auch eher wie ein Straßenmusiker, der sich irgendwo niederläßt und darauf baut, daß seine Lieder so gut sind, daß er nicht weggejagt wird.

Nochmals zurück zu unserer Skulptur "Bauzaun", die wir zu den Skulptur-Projekten in der Innenstadt von Münster entwickelten: Wir waren nun wirklich nicht damit zufrieden, wie sich dieser Platz, diese Restfläche im Herzen der Stadt präsentierte. Da wurde ein wirklich ziemlich unangenehmes Kunstwerk sehr aufwendig installiert (ich meine diese Fahnen), um die Leere irgendwie nicht zu deutlich werden zu lassen. Da wurde einer alten Kirche eine rasant bespoilerte Kaufhausfassade und ein Kaufhausneubau entgegengestellt, deren räumliche oder architektonische Bezüge nicht nachzuvollziehen sind. Da wurden natürlich auch Bänke um die Bäume herumgruppiert – diese Fertigteile halt – und der Fußboden historisierend gepflastert. Eine typisch deutsche Fußgängerzone eben und eine verpaßte Chance dazu.

Wir wollten dann mit unserem Kasten-Bauzaun eine Möglichkeit der Platzüberquerung schaffen, ohne daß man Teil dieses zweifelhaften Ensembles ist, also wie über den Platz gebeamt wird. Wir gaben also all diesen hier versammelten Welten bewußt eine weitere dazu, so daß irgendwie gar nichts mehr zueinander paßte. Die Tragik der Geschichte war dann aber, daß es möglicherweise nicht deutlich genug wurde, was wir eigentlich wollten und manche das "Bunte Blechfahnenensemble", zwischen das sich unser Kastenhaus schlängelte (gerne auch "wurstelte"), als Teil unseres Kunstwerkes sahen, so, als hätten wir die Dinger als Dekor unseres Kastenhauses selbst gebaut. Ich glaube, diese Art von

Modell (Gartenturm, Schloß Nord-
kirchen), 1998
Gips, Harz, Knetfigur,
27 x 20 x 20 cm
Skulptur-Biennale 1999 im
Münsterland

FM: *Your next project for the 1999 Sculpture Biennial actually does allude to the aspects you've mentioned. Your proposal for a small 18th-century-style rotunda on the "periphery" of the baroque gardens of Schloß Nordkirchen in the southern part of the Münsterland region is an attempt to establish a perceptible link between the past and the present. In contrast to the Disneyland-style appearance of the castle and the gardens themselves, which look as if they had been "frozen" in time, this—as yet unrestored—rotunda remains one of the few authentic references to the age of the property as a whole. The tooth of time has clearly gnawed at the substance of the little rotunda. The recent construction of stables nearby has also contributed to the fundamental changes in the historical situation. The first phase of your proposed project calls for a restoration of the area to its original condition, to include the removal of these new structures, followed by renovation of the rotunda, during which colored, molded window panes will be mounted and a standing sculpture will be installed in the interior.*

BH: *In the course of our joint inspection of the castles, grounds and gardens in Lüdinghausen, Nordkirchen and Westerwinkel we experienced the sense of a "journey through time" you mention on our return trip to Münster—I think it was just outside of Ascheberg. As you have told us, other artists you have accompanied were also astounded at the sight of a typical residential development hidden behind an earthen embankment in the landscape. The situation is different. Noise reduction is more important than concealment from view, and the antenna towers above the embankment. Efforts in support of spatial and aesthetic improvements such as those undertaken in adjacent neighborhoods are given low priority.*

As we walked through the parks and gardens we took notice of the familiar proportions of the two round towers (several of our beverage-case houses, including the ones in Aasee and Münster, had similar dimensions). These round towers originally formed the boundary between the landscaped gardens and the landscape itself. Later structural additions have obstructed the view of the entire surrounding area. The situation is no longer recognizable as an interface. Some of the doors and windows have been bricked up. Our initial work will involve a traditional sculptural technique: removing excess material.

Eingriff war dann in Bonn vor der Bundeskunsthalle klarer formuliert und die Ironie wurde deutlicher.

Ob das für uns problematisch ist, wenn beispielsweise Japaner unsere Kästen als eigenwillige Gußform aus der Hand des Künstlers, anstatt aus dem Pfandsystem des Getränkehandels interpretieren: Um bei dem Bild vom Musiker zu bleiben: Wir spielen unser Instrument, als das wir es erfunden haben, und wir spielen darauf Eigenkompositionen. Ich frage ja auch keinen Inder, ob er seine Sitar selbst erfunden hat, nur weil sie nicht aussieht wie eine Gitarre... Darüber hinaus: Jedes Material, so auch unsere Kästen, sind nichts als Werkzeuge, möglicherweise von sehr speziellem Eigenleben, aber letztlich tump, weil sie in ihrer Anwesenheit ständig auf unser irdisches Dasein verweisen wollen.

FM: Euer neuestes Projekt anläßlich der Skulptur-Biennale 1999 verweist ja in der Tat auf die von Dir genannten Aspekte. Euer Vorschlag für einen kleinen Rundbau aus dem 18. Jahrhundert in der "Peripherie" der barocken Gartenanlagen von Schloß Nordkirchen im südlichen Münsterland versucht sinnfällig die Verknüpfung von Gestern und Heute. Gegenüber des Disneyland-ähnlichen Zustandes des Schlosses und der Gartenanlagen selbst, in der die Zeit "eingefroren" erscheint, ist dieser – noch nicht restaurierte – Rundturm einer der wenigen authentischen Verweise auf das Alter der Gesamtanlage: deutlich hat der "Zahn der Zeit" das Türmchen verfallen lassen, angrenzende Neubauten von Pferdeställen haben darüber hinaus die historische Situation grundlegend verändert. Im Rahmen Eures Projektvorschlages seht Ihr in einem ersten Schritt eine Rekonstruktion des originalen Zustandes vor, d.h. die Entfernung dieser Neubauten, um daraufhin den Rundturm mit farbig gegossenen Fensterscheiben und einer Bodenarbeit im Innern zu verändern.

BH: Bei unserer ersten gemeinsamen Besichtigung der Schlösser Lüdinghausen, Nordkirchen und Westerwinkel und deren Gärten und Anlagen, wurde uns die von Dir angesprochene "Zeitreise" auf der Rückfahrt nach Münster, ich glaube kurz vor Ascheberg, noch einmal deutlich vor Augen geführt. Deinen Berichten zufolge staunten auch andere, Dich begleitende Künstler über eine typische Wohnsiedlung, die sich hinter einem Erdwall in der Gegend versteckt. Die Situation ist anders: Lärmbeseitigung geht vor Sichtbehinderung, die Antenne ragt ja über den

FM: In my view, this is exactly the opportunity for art—particularly in public space—to do what it can do best today: make historical or psychological structures visible again and transpose them into the here and now. After all, the historical view from the round tower into the baroque landscape garden is replaced by the "nebulous", color-oriented gaze of the viewer into a surrounding landscape that is neither place nor non-place but simply "area".

WW: What is really at issue here is the idea of making something that already exists visible once again. We must try to intervene as little but as effectively as possible in order to avoid the appearance of a conglomeration of fragments. Of course our focus on the tower—or rotunda, as you call it—also relates to our interest in this kind of architecture; and we do see a link between the round tower and our beverage-case installations. We are concerned with the formal characteristics of a sculptural or architectural structure and its component parts. What can be done with them and in what way it can be done is governed by an artistic process. And the tower reflects a special relationship of interior to exterior space and vice-versa, since it is a building itself yet describes, with its two adjacent doors, a transitional situation. It is easy to imagine young baroque ladies changing into their hunting clothes inside the tower [. . .]. So the tower was a kind of dressing room, a container for a special kind of intimacy. By filling the window openings with our transparent—in this case bluish—shimmering plastic material, which we used, for example, for the "same-same Madonnas", we wanted to create a new interior situation that would nonetheless allude to this particular form of intimacy. The clouded view into the interior is similar to the effect of sunglasses on vision, and the use of sunglasses can ultimately be a form of intimacy as well. [. . .] By the way, we are less interested in the tower as functional architecture and more in its role as Festarchitektur, a term attributable to the architect Rudolf Schwarz, who meant it to denote a certain "festive" or solemn quality.

FM: The relationship between interior and exterior and thus, in a narrower sense,

Modell (Berg, Schloß Nordkirchen), 1998
Zement, Ziegelsteine, Gips, 50 x 60 x 60 cm
Skulptur-Biennale 1999 im Münsterland

Wall, räumliche und gestalterische Anstrengungen wie in der unmittelbaren Nachbarschaft stehen hinten an.

Während wir durch die Parkanlagen gingen, bemerkten wir die uns sehr vertrauten Proportionen (einige Kastenhäuser, z.B. Aasee, Münster, hatten ähnliche Maße) der beiden Rundtürme. Diese Rundtürme bildeten ursprünglich die Grenze zwischen gestalteter Gartenanlage und Landschaft, durch nachträgliche Anbauten ist eine freie Rundsicht behindert, die Situation als Schnittstelle nicht mehr nachvollziehbar. Fenster und Türen sind teilweise zugemauert. Bei unseren ersten Maßnahmen bedienen wir uns einer Methode der Bildhauerei: Abtragen der überflüssigen Masse.

FM: Für mich ist dies genau die Chance, die Kunst heute – insbesondere im Öffentlichen Raum – leisten kann: Sichtbarmachung geschichtlicher oder psychologischer Strukturen und deren Transformation in das Jetzt, denn der historische Blick aus dem Rundturm in die Gartenanlagen des Barock wird ersetzt durch den "verschwommenen", farbig gefaßten Blick des zeitgenössischen Betrachters in eine Umgebung, die weder Ort noch Unort ist, sondern einfach nur "Gegend".

WW: Eigentlich geht es hier mehr darum, bereits vorhandenes wieder sichtbar zu machen. Wir müssen versuchen, möglichst wenige und gezielte Eingriffe vorzunehmen, um den Charakter der Gegend, des Ortes nicht zu verklittern. Daß wir uns den Turm – oder Rundbau, wie du ihn nennst – , als zentrales Objekt vorgenommen haben, hat natürlich auch mit unserem Interesse für solche Architekturen zu tun; und eine Parallele vom Rundturm zu unseren Kastenhäusern sehen wir schon. Uns interessieren formale Eigenheiten eines skulpturalen oder architektonischen Gebildes und seiner Elemente. Das, was man damit in welcher Weise machen kann, obliegt einem künstlerischen Prozeß. Und der Turmbau spiegelt ein besonderes Verhältnis vom Innen- zum Außenraum und umgekehrt, da er selbst zwar Gebäude ist, jedoch mit zwei nebeneinander liegenden Türen ausgestattet, eine Übergangssituation beschreibt. Man kann sich sehr gut vorstellen, wie die jungen barocken Damen sich darin zur Jagd umkleideten... Also war der Turm möglicherweise so eine Art Umkleidekabine, ein Gefäß für eine besondere Intimität. Das Eingießen der Fensteröffnungen mit unserem zum Beispiel bei den

between the private and the public was also a determining aspect of your Scobalit-Raum, an installation you realised in 1997. A conceptual extension of the beverage-case-house projects, so to speak, this work was also a walk-through piece that connected a total of three storeys.

BH: The second floor of the Galerie Voges und Deisen has been used as an exhibition room ever since the gallery opened. The office and sanitary facilities were located on the third floor. Shortly before our exhibition in the fall of 97, the gallery expanded to incorporate the ground floor, which had previously been rented out.

Our installation was to establish a connection to all three floors: The drain in the washbasin on the third floor was diverted into a drainpipe installed between the ceiling and the floor on the

Stellprobe für Skulptur. Projekte in Münster, 1997

second floor. Whenever the washbasin was used, you could hear and see the water flowing through this pipe, which was molded and then cast in transparent acrylic resin. We also sawed a hole with a diameter of 80 cm through the floor of the second storey. There, we constructed a transparent space elevated slightly on a pedestal out of corrugated PBC (Scobalit. The outside and inside of the installation could be entered only through separate building doors. The hole leading to the second floor was located inside this space.

FM: Aside from the aspect of the relationship between interior and exterior space, your interest in developing aesthetic forms from existing functional elements also plays a role here. I would go even further and suggest that your works "rub against the grain" of the traditional concept of sculpture, and that you are attempting to go beyond standards of form, function, material and message "prescribed" by the history of art at the close of the 20th century, without denying the existence of that tradition.

"Same-Same-Madonnen" verwendeten, transparent – hier bläulich – schimmernden Kunststoffmaterial soll eine neue Innenraum-Situation schaffen, die aber zugleich auf diese Form der Intimität hinweist. Die Trübung des Blickes beim "Hinausschauen" kommt etwa der Verwendung einer Sonnenbrille am nächsten, deren Anwendung ja letztlich auch eine Form der Intimität bedeuten kann... Es ist übrigens weniger der Turm als Zweckarchitektur, was uns hierbei interessiert, eher schon Festarchitektur, ein Begriff, der auf den Architekten Rudolf Schwarz zurückgeht, der aber nicht "feste" Architektur meint, sondern Fest im Sinne von Feierlichkeit.

FM: Das Verhältnis von Innen und Außen und damit auch im engeren Sinne von Privat und Öffentlich bestimmte ja auch Euren "Scobalit-Raum", eine Installation, die Ihr 1997 realisiert habt: Gleichsam als konzeptuelle Fortführung der Kastenhaus-Projekte war diese Arbeit begehbar und verknüpfte insgesamt drei Stockwerke miteinander.

BH: Seit ihrem Bestehen wurde die 1. Etage der Galerie Voges und Deisen als Ausstellungsraum genutzt, Büro und die sanitären Anlagen waren im Obergeschoß untergebracht. Kurz vor unserer Ausstellung im Herbst 97 erweiterte sich die Galerie auf das bis dahin vermietete Erdgeschoß.

Unsere Installation sah vor, eine Verbindung zu allen drei Etagen zu schaffen: Vom 2. Stockwerk wurde der Abfluß des Handwaschbeckens in ein zwischen Decke und Fußboden der 1. Etage installiertes Abflußrohr umgeleitet. Bei Benutzung des Waschbeckens sah und hörte man den Wasserfluß in diesem modellierten und anschließend in durchsichtigem Harz gegossenen Rohr.

Weiter sägten wir in den Fußboden der 1. Etage ein Loch von 80 cm Durchmesser zum Erdgeschoß. Dort bauten wir aus handelsüblichem Well-PVC (Scobalit) einen durch ein Podest leicht erhöhten, transparenten Raum. Außen und Innen der Installation konnte jeweils nur durch separate Hauseingänge betreten werden. Das Loch zur 1. Etage befand sich im Inneren.

FM: Neben dem Aspekt des Verhältnisses von Innen- und Außenraum spielte auch hier der Aspekt der Entwicklung ästhetischer Formen aus vorhandenen Funktionsformen eine Rolle. Weiterführend glaube ich, daß Eure Arbeiten sich am traditionellen Skulptur-Begriff "reiben" und Ihr versucht, durch die Kunstgeschichte

As an art historian, I find affinities between the Handtuch-Arbeiten (Towel Pieces), for example, and the early works of Richard Serra from the sixties and seventies, sculptures in which the hard material—steel, a difficult substance to work—was in a sense negated and the forms of soft materials—rubber, fabrics, etc.—were "copied".

Several of your beverage-case installations—especially the Lichtspielhaus (Movie Theatre)—evoke (by virtue of the fantastical light effects achieved through the use of different kinds of artificial illumination or natural light and through their transparency, which makes the "walls" seem to become flowing interfaces between the interior and the exterior, compelling the viewer / visitor to redefine his or her location after every movement) visual and aesthetic experiences that call to mind the glass and mirror pavilions of Dan Graham.

It appears quite clear, however—and I think this is the real point—that you have taken these aspects of western post-war art a decisive step further. It seems to me that only a few artists of your generation have succeeded as you have in translating these artistic "prescriptions" into terms relevant to the nineties. We find a good example of what I mean in the variations on the neo-classical bust of Voltaire. They are not arranged in orderly rows and columns but as figures in a table-soccer game—a scheme that has little meaning in art but is crucial to an athlete—as participants in a dialogue, indeed in a competitive relationship with one another. Voltaire conversing with himself about himself!

BH: *In applying our "same-same" process to a toy doll, we wanted to put a meaningful limit on what seems to be its infinite potential for multiplication by arranging it in the configuration of a table-football game. In the case of the Voltaire bust, we made a number of attempts to replicate it. Ultimately, one transformation turned out to be quite singular. [. . .]*

Of course when we received the first requests to design a movie theatre made of beverage cases, we were interested in finding out how about the behaviour of light inside and outside the space, in seeing how a film or the action of a film would be transported into outside space through its reflections and in identifying changes on the inside resulting from different-sized audiences and varying weather conditions. The movie theatre opened with Andy Warhol's film Mario Banana.

des zu Ende gehenden 20. Jahrhunderts "vorgegebene" Standards in Bezug auf Form, Funktion, Material und Aussage hin weiterzuentwickeln, ohne aber diese Tradition leugnen zu wollen.

Die "Handtuch-Arbeiten" beispielsweise knüpfen für mich als Kunsthistoriker an die frühen Arbeiten von Richard Serra aus den 60er und 70er Jahren an, in denen das harte Material – schwer bearbeitbarer Stahl – gleichsam negiert wurde und die Formen weicher Materialien – Gummi, Stoff usw. – "kopiert" wurden.

Weiterhin evozieren einige Kastenhäuser – insbesondere z.B. das "Lichtspielhaus" in Berlin – mit Ihren phantastischen Lichteffekten bei unterschiedlicher künstlicher Beleuchtung oder natürlicher Belichtung, mit Ihrer Transparenz, in der die "Wände" gleichsam zu fließenden Schnittstellen zwischen Außen und Innen werden, in denen der Betrachter/Besucher seinen Standort bei jeder Bewegung neu zu definieren hat, visuelle und ästhetische Seherfahrungen, die vergleichbar sind mit den Glas- und Spiegelpavillons von Dan Graham.

Allerdings – und das scheint mir das entscheidende zu sein – habt Ihr diese Aspekte der westlichen Nachkriegskunst entscheidend weiterentwickelt, ich glaube, Ihr habt es wie wenige Künstler Furer Generation geschafft, diese künstlerischen "Vorgaben" sinnfällig in die 90er Jahre zu transformieren. Ein gutes Beispiel dafür sind etwa auch die Variationen der klassizistischen Portrait-Büste Voltaires, die nicht in "Reih und Glied", sondern entsprechend den – für die Kunst belanglosen, für den Sport aber alles entscheidenden – Formationen des Tischfußballes in ein dialogisches, ja konkurrierendes Verhältnis zueinander treten: Voltaire kommuniziert mit sich und über sich selbst!

BH: Bei der Anwendung unseres "Same-Same"-Verfahrens an einer Spielzeugpuppe wollten wir deren scheinbar endlos fortsetzbaren Multiplikatoren durch die Anordnung zu einem "Tischfußball" eine sinnvolle Begrenzung geben. Für die Büste des "Voltaire" gab es mehrere Versuche, ihn zu multiplizieren. Letztlich blieb eine Transformation singulär...

Natürlich waren wir bei ersten Anfragen, ein Kino aus Wasserkästen zu entwerfen, sofort interessiert, wie sich das Licht innerhalb und außerhalb des Raumes verhalten, wie der Film oder die Handlung des Filmes sich durch seine Reflexion in den Außenraum transportieren würde, und an den jeweiligen Verän-

Stellprobe Kastenhaus 2640.15
(Lichtspielhaus Berlin), 1998,
Frankfurt/Naxoshalle

WW: *Points of contact with significant positions of contemporary artists do emerge again and again. Yet I am convinced that what we do differs a priori from what others are doing in several ways and that different motivations underlie our work—not to mention distinctions with respect to the material character of our sculptures, their form, the methods we use, and so on. [. . .] We should also point out that the large number of competing and corresponding media of the visual arts has resulted in a considerable rise in standards in the late nineties for those who work in a single discipline—namely sculpture—only. Thus the question we must answer cannot be "How can I distinguish myself from the others", but rather "What can sculpture do that other media cannot? Where are the boundaries? Where is the break in the bond that ties us to the canon of sculpture?" And that is why we also experiment with different functions (movie theatres, bus stops, etcetera). Our beverage-case installations thus explore the modern quest for autonomy in the visual arts.*

FM: *What does the traditional concept of sculpture actually mean to you? By that I mean working in and with three-dimensional space—as autonomous sculpture or as context-related installation—within the ensemble of the competitive classical disciplines of architecture, sculpture and painting?*

WW: *Sure—the point is to develop a concept of sculpture that can take us further. The word "sculpture" comes from the Latin sculpere, which can be translated as chiseling, carving [. . .] or perhaps even forming. Chiseling and carving are to be understood in a more abstract sense as activities in which something is taken away until something else is left—in contrast to the work of sculptor who models, adding clay or some other material to arrive at a final product. Those are really the registers of sculpture and modelling. We, Berthold and I, ordinarily operate within this framework, although more and more in the sense that the processes of removal or addition can be understood as a way of organising material masses (as malleable, "plastic" masses). In some cases we do no more than set up conditions so that something specific can take place, something that relates to the concept of sculpture. In other words, when everything is in place, the sculpture is finished.*

derungen im Inneren bei unterschiedlichem Publikumsandrang und Wetterlage. Das Lichtspielhaus eröffnete mit Andy Warhol's Film "Mario Banana".

WW: Sicher gibt es immer wieder Berührungspunkte mit prägnanten Positionen zeitgenössischer Künstler. Ich bin jedoch davon überzeugt, daß sich das, was wir machen, schon im Ansatz um einiges unterscheidet von anderen und andere Beweggründe vorliegen – von der Unterscheidung hinsichtlich der Materialität der Arbeiten, der Formgebung, der Methode etc. ganz zu schweigen... Außerdem ist gegen Ende der 90er Jahre durch die Vielzahl der miteinander konkurrierenden und korrespondierenden Medien innerhalb der Bildenden Kunst die Meßlatte doch ziemlich hoch gelegt, wenn man sich auf eine Disziplin – nämlich Skulptur – beschränkt, so daß die Fragestellung für uns nicht lauten kann: "Wie unterscheide ich mich von anderen", sondern viel mehr: "Was kann Skulptur gegenüber anderen Medien, wo sind Grenzen, wo zerreißt das Band, das mit dem Kanon von Skulptur verbindet?" – Deshalb machen wir auch solche Experimente mit unterschiedlichen Funktionen (Kino, Bushaltestelle etc.), unsere Kastenhäuser befragen damit das moderne Autonomiebestreben von Bildender Kunst.

FM: Welche Bedeutung hat für Euch eigentlich der traditionelle Skulptur-Begriff, das heißt dreidimensionales Arbeiten im Raum – als autonome Skulptur ebenso wie als kontextbezogene Installation – im Konkurrenzgefüge der klassischen Gattungen von Architektur, Skulptur und Malerei?

WW: Es geht um die Herausarbeitung eines Skulptur-Begriffes, der weiterführend sein kann. Das Wort Skulptur stammt ja vom lateinischen „sculpere", was übersetzt werden kann mit meißeln, schnitzen... oder vielleicht auch bilden. Meißeln und Schnitzen sind Tätigkeiten, die aber auch abstrakter zu verstehen sind als Tätigkeiten, die etwas wegnehmen, bis etwas anderes übrigbleibt – im Gegensatz zum Plastiker, der Ton oder andere Massen anträgt, bis etwas entsteht. Das sind eigentlich die Register der Bildhauerei und des Plastizierens. Wir, also Berthold und ich, bewegen uns normalerweise innerhalb dieses Rahmens, jedoch immer mehr so, daß das Wegnehmen oder das Hinzufügen als eine Art Organisieren der Massen (im Sinne von plastischen Massen) zu verstehen ist. Manchmal stellen wir auch nur Bedingungen bereit, damit etwas Bestimmtes stattfinden kann, was mit dem Begriff Skulptur zusammenhängt. Also: Wenn alles an seinem Platz ist, ist die Skulptur fertig.

This is the one aspect of sculpere. Another interesting aspect of removal is the fact that a sculpture may be created through the process of removal, meaning that no recognisable material object remains. What is left is only the "essence" and configuration of things that already existed, which now become visible through the removal of others but also take on enormous sculptural qualities as a result, although in a utilitarian sense they are merely telephone boxes, for example.

It is at this point that the space-creating power of things appears, and they become—I would say—very significant.

If one were to move across a flat plain without elevations or depressions, it would be impossible to perceive space. Only when something stands out can one recognise distances, proximity, height—size in all of its dimensions—and experience space (and one's own existence, for that matter). But when there is too much standing about in confusion, space recedes, things lose their object character (that which distinguishes them) and their essence (that which is inherent in them), and they grow dumb. And now we are talking once again about urban space and all of its junk and the longing for something to focus one's gaze upon—perhaps even a sculpture. These ideas aren't really so new at all.

Beyond that, we are trying to explore the capacity of sculpture to assume a social dimension—though not in the sense of social work or some kind of helper syndrome. So when we do a project in conjunction with a rehabilitation centre or work, as we are doing now, with blind youth (who by the way have modelled very beautiful heads with great character as wall reliefs for a new beverage-case house that is to be erected outdoors on their school grounds), or when our beverage-case houses are utilised in a very concrete way, then there is a social dimension involved, but in the sense of "working together on something", developing something and accepting certain aspects that may tend to be alien to us, which is actually the case in our teamwork.

This is an experiment, an attempt to explore modern art's quest for autonomy in a serious way. It is not public service. You can't plan what is going to happen one hundred per cent. But getting involved with something like this every once in a while has its advantages: It keeps us relaxed and gives us a chance to meet people [...]

Dies ist der eine Teil von sculpere. Ein interessanter Aspekt des Wegnehmens ist auch, daß möglicherweise eine Skulptur dadurch entstehen kann, daß etwas weggenommen wird, also gar kein materialer Gegenstand erkennbar wird, sondern nur noch die "Wesenhaftigkeit" und Anordnung bereits vorhandener Dinge durch das Entfernen anderer sichtbar gemacht werden, die dadurch aber enorme skulpturale Qualitäten bekommen, von ihrer Dienlichkeit her aber z.B. nur Telephonhäuschen sind.

Dann tritt die raumschaffende Kraft der Dinge zutage, und sie werden – in meinen Augen – bedeutsam.

Würde man sich auf einer flachen Ebene ohne Erhebungen und Löcher bewegen, wäre der Raum nicht zu erfassen; erst, wenn irgendwo etwas steht, kann man Entfernungen, Nähe, Höhe, Größe in ihren Verhältnissen erkennen und Raum (und meinetwegen auch die eigene Existenz) erfahren. Wenn aber zu viel zu wirr herumsteht, verschließt sich die Räumlichkeit, die Dinge verändern ihre Gegenständlichkeit (das, was sie entgegenstellen) und ihre Wesenhaftigkeit (das, was ihnen innewohnt), und sie sind tumb. Hier geht es dann wieder um den städtischen Raum mit all dem Gcrümpel und der Sehnsucht nach dem Focussieren des eigenen Blickes – vielleicht auf eine Skulptur. Diese Überlegungen sind nicht neu.

Wir versuchen darüber hinaus auszuloten, inwieweit Skulptur eine soziale Dimension haben kann – und zwar nicht im Sinne von Sozialarbeit und Helfersyndrom. Wenn wir also ein Projekt in Zusammenarbeit mit einem Rehabilitationszentrum machen oder etwa aktuell mit blinden Jugendlichen kooperieren (die übrigens sehr schöne und charaktervolle Köpfe modelliert haben, als Module für eine neue Entwicklung einer begehbaren Skulptur) oder unsere Kastenhäuser teilweise sehr konkret genutzt werden, so geht es um eine soziale Dimension, jedoch mehr im Sinne von "zusammen an etwas arbeiten, etwas entwickeln und bestimmte, eher fremde Aspekte zulassen", was ja auch auf unsere Teamarbeit zutrifft.

Dies ist ein Experiment, ein Versuch, die Autonomiebestrebungen moderner Kunst ernsthaft zu befragen und kein öffentlicher Dienst; was dann passiert, kann man nicht hundertprozentig planen. Aber, sich ab und zu auf so etwas einlassen, hat auch einen ganz anderen Vorteil: Man bleibt schön locker und lernt die Leute kennen…

oben Kastenhaus 2640.15 (Lichtspielhaus, Innenansicht), 1998, Berlin, Künstlerhaus Bethanien, The Cinema Project

rechts Kastenhaus 2640.15 (Lichtspielhaus, Detailansicht), 1998

rechts Kastenhaus 2640.15 (Lichtspielhaus, Innenansicht), 1998, Berlin, Künstlerhaus Bethanien, The Cinema Project

Kastenhaus 2640.15 (Lichtspielhaus, Innenansicht), 1998, Berlin, Künstlerhaus Bethanien, The Cinema Project

Wolfgang Ullrich   ***STOCKED GOODS AS FESTIVE ARCHITECTURE***
The Beverage-Case Structures of Wolfgang Winter and
Berthold Hörbelt

Wolfgang Winter and Berthold Hörbelt have been building beverage-case structu-res since 1996. Working at a number of locations, they have stacked hundreds of (empty) beverage cases at different public sites for periods of several days, weeks or months, arranging them in rows to form straight, convex or concave walls whose final configurations define the structure of a pavilion or a kiosk. Because of the handgrips built into the cases, the walls of these structures are full of openings, which nevertheless form regular patterns. Produced in standard dimensions, the cases are actually modules which fit snugly together and differ only by virtue of their various colours.

Admittedly, constructing a building out of similar or even identical building blocks is nothing new. The pyramids of Egypt were erected with stones that had previously been cut as nearly as possible to the same size. Bricks and concrete wall sections have been manufactured in standards sizes for many years. Yet Winter's and Hörbelt's structures comprised of beverage cases cannot really be compared to these. Whereas bricks and concrete wall sections are intended sole-ly for the purpose of being joined together to form walls, floors and ceilings, these cases are ordinarily found only on beverage suppliers' delivery trucks, in bevera-ge markets or wholesale outlets—stacked in rows like saleable goods, as contai-ners suitable for the safe and practical transportation of bottles. Despite its solid appearance, the beverage-case structure clearly has the appearance of a tempo-rary affair, since we are well aware how quickly such stacks and towers of bever-age cases can diminish in size.

In the case of the structures erected by Wolfgang Winter and Berthold Hörbelt, however, the beverage cases are not displayed as saleable commodities but have instead been extracted from the cycle of commerce and transformed into building material. In addition, the structures themselves are assigned a definite function, serving, for example, as cinemas or bus-stop shelters. This makes it pos-

Wolfgang Ullrich **STAPELWARE ALS FESTARCHITEKTUR**
Zu den Kastenhäusern von Wolfgang Winter und Berthold Hörbelt

Seit 1996 bauen Wolfgang Winter und Berthold Hörbelt Kastenhäuser. An mittlerweile zahlreichen Orten stapelten sie, jeweils für einige Tage, Wochen oder Monate, auf einem öffentlichen Platz etliche hundert (leere) Wasserkästen aufeinander und reihten die Stapel zu geraden, konvexen oder konkaven Wänden, bis sich schließlich Gebilde in der Form eines Pavillons oder Kiosks ergeben. Die Wände dieser Häuser sind dank der Trageöffnungen der Kästen vielfach, aber regelmäßig durchbrochen. Aufgrund der genormten Maße der Kästen handelt es sich bei ihnen um fugenlos zueinander passende Module, die sich höchstens in ihrer jeweiligen Farbe unterscheiden.

Freilich: Ein Haus aus ähnlichen oder gar identischen Bausteinen zu errichten, ist nichts Neues. Schon die Pyramiden der Ägypter wurden aus Steinen aufgetürmt, die zuvor auf die möglichst selbe Größe zugeschnitten worden waren; auch Ziegelsteine und Betonplatten sind bereits seit langem genormt. Dennoch sind die aus Wasserkästen zusammengesetzten Häuser von Winter/Hörbelt damit nicht vergleichbar. Während Ziegelsteine oder Betonplatten allein dem Zweck genügen, zu Mauern und Decken verbunden zu werden, die im übrigen meist verputzt sind, begegnen die Wasserkästen hier zunächst nicht anders als im Lieferwagen des Getränkehändlers, im Getränkemarkt oder im Großhandel: Wie Waren gestapelt und gereiht, als Behältnisse, die zum praktikablen und sicheren Transport von Flaschen geeignet sind. So massiv ein Kastenhaus auch wirken mag, so deutlich erscheint es dennoch als eine temporäre Angelegenheit, da man weiß, wie rasch normalerweise die Stapel und Türme von Wasserkästen wachsen und sich wieder dezimieren.

Bei den Häusern von Wolfgang Winter und Berthold Hörbelt werden die Wasserkästen jedoch gar nicht als Ware offeriert; vielmehr sind sie dem Handelskreislauf entzogen und mutieren zu Baumaterial. Die Häuser selbst bekommen zudem eine klare Funktion zugewiesen und fungieren etwa als Kino oder Buswarteunterstand. Das ermöglicht einen anderen Blick auf die Kästen, und was im

sible to view the cases in a very different way, and what goes unnoticed at the beverage market is suddenly the focus of celebration. In their customary setting, stacks of beverage cases are hardly ever perceived as structures—much less sculptures—in their own right; and shopping is not the kind of contemplative activity in which one is likely to appreciate the rapport

Kastenhaus 1128.8/639.9 (Bauzaun), 1997 Münster, Salzstraße, Skulptur. Projekte in Münster

created through the union of uniformly shaped beverage cases. Only when they are converted into a building material that is demonstrably stable yet still allows the passage of light are we confronted with formal-aesthetic aspects and the material properties of such a mass-produced product.

In a shop, by way of contrast, the presence of stacks of identical goods is meant to suggest overabundance. The idea is to impress with huge quantities. More importantly, this approach tends to minimise the value of the single item; it then begins to look less expensive, and consumers becomes less resistant to making larger purchases. The act of making a purchase tends to be taken for granted and takes on a serial character; it is not staged as a special or unique event. Accordingly, the presentation of stacked goods has been one of the most popular of all marketing methods since the infancy of serial production, as is clearly evident in photographs of department stores taken around the turn of the century. Artists have been engaged for some time in the pursuit of the perceptual changes that take place with regard to things that are not presented singly but rather in series—stacked, in rows or in piles. As early as 1931, Amedée Ozenfant included in his book Die Grundlagen der modernen Kunst an illustration of a showcase window in which tennis racquets and balls are arranged in serial presentation. What he recognised as an important means of creating patterns and thus as a preliminary stage of abstraction—the importance of the individual piece is subordinate to the ornamental effect of the rapport—had of course already been the focus of criticism by Siegfried Kracauer several years before. In his essay entitled "Das Ornament der Masse," published in 1927, Kracauer points out that even the individual human being is instrumentalised to a certain extent as a part of an abstract-geometric pattern at mass events and thus robbed of his individuality. His

Getränkemarkt zu kurz kommt, wird auf einmal zelebriert. Dort nämlich nimmt man aufgetürmte Wasserkästen kaum einmal als eigenständige Gebilde oder gar Skulpturen wahr; außerdem ist Einkaufen nicht so kontemplativ, daß man auf den Rapport achtet, der im Verbund gleichartiger Wasserkästen entsteht. Erst wenn diese zu einem Baustoff werden, der sich als stabil und zugleich lichtfreundlich bewährt, fallen formal- ästhetische Aspekte sowie die Materialeigenschaften eines solchen Massenprodukts auf.

In einem Laden hingegen soll das Stapeln von jeweils identischer Ware Überfluß suggerieren; man setzt darauf, mit Masse zu imponieren. Vor allem aber will man den Wert des Einzelstücks dadurch minimieren; es wirkt dann billiger, was die Kaufschwelle senkt. Der Kaufakt wird beiläufig und selbst seriell; er soll gerade nicht als etwas Besonderes oder Einmaliges inszeniert werden. Entsprechend gehört Stapelware seit den Anfängen serieller Produktion zu den beliebtesten Marketingmethoden, wie Fotografien von Kaufhäusern belegen, die aus der Zeit der letzten Jahrhundertwende stammen.

Umgekehrt gehen Künstler schon länger den Wahrnehmungswandlungen nach, die sich gegenüber etwas vollziehen, das nicht einzeln, sondern in Serie – gestapelt, gereiht oder gehäuft – präsentiert wird. Bereits 1931 bildete Amédée Ozenfant in seinem Buch "Die Grundlagen der modernen Kunst" ein Schaufenster ab, in dem Tennisschläger und -bälle nach dem Prinzip der Serialität arrangiert sind. Was hier als wesentliches Mittel der Mustererzeugung und damit als Vorstufe zur Abstraktion erkannt wird – die Bedeutung des Einzelstücks ordnet sich dem Ornament des Rapports unter – , wurde kurz zuvor freilich schon von Siegfried Kracauer mit Argwohn betrachtet. In seinem 1927 publizierten Essay "Das Ornament der Masse" gibt er zu bedenken, daß bei Massenveranstaltungen auch der einzelne Mensch zum Teil eines abstrakt-geometrischen Musters instrumentalisiert werde und dabei seiner Individualität verlustig gehe. Berühmt sind seine Bemerkungen zu den "Tillergirls", einer erfolgreichen Revue-Gruppe der zwanziger Jahre: "Diese Produkte der amerikanischen Zerstreuungsfabriken sind keine einzelnen Mädchen mehr, sondern unauflösliche Mädchenkomplexe, deren Bewegungen mathematische Demonstrationen sind. (...) Der Regelmässigkeit ihrer Muster jubelt die durch die Tribünen gegliederte Menge zu."

remarks on the "Tillergirls", a successful revue group of the twenties, have become famous: "These products of American entertainment factories are no longer human individuals; instead they have become indissoluble girl complexes whose movements are mathematical demonstrations. [...] The crowd, structured by the configuration of the stands, jubilantly applauds the regularity of their formations." The focus of this unequivocal judgement by Kracauer and many other culture critics—the idea of human beings relating to one another in the age of factory production only in constellations of patterns—was approached in a much more sober yet grandiose style by American Pop Artists several decades later. Andy Warhol was one of the artists most closely concerned with the principle of serial production, and he demonstrated the phenomena of technical and media reproducibility along with its specific myths and materials in his art. Soup cans and Coca-Cola bottles were his mass-produced products, which he presented as mass-produced products, and he used repetition to turn Mao's face into a wallpaper pattern. In most cases, Warhol's studies in seriality were confined to two-dimensional works. His famous Brillo Boxes of 1964 are the exception, along with other packaging boxes—each reproduced by Warhol himself—which could only be stacked four or five layers high, however. Although methods of merchandise presentation were adapted and made recognisable as such in this case, Warhol's work did not involve a genuine exploration of the possibilities for the use of seriality in the field of sculpture and art in public space.

Only in recent years have other artists besides Wolfgang Winter and Berthold Hörbelt begun to close this gap. Katharina Fritsch, for example, made the serial arrangement of goods the subject of several of her works, introducing clearance-sale tables and merchandise display racks into the context of art. The most famous of these works was a rack displaying 288 yellow-painted Madonna figures stacked in nine layers (Merchandise Display with Madonnas, 1987/89).

Stephan Huber is concerned with the sense of alienation things experience as a consequence of repetition. He frequently arranges collections of open tool boxes to form columns or entire walls, and the patterns created in this way make it difficult to identify the original function of the basic module. Unlike the beverage-case, the object stacked in Huber's installations is a serially produced item

Was hier und bei vielen anderen Kulturkritikern eine eindeutige Wertung erfuhr – Menschen begegnen einander im Zeitalter der Fabriken nur noch in Musterkonstellationen – , wurde viel nüchterner und dafür im großen Stil einige Jahrzehnte später von der amerikanischen Pop-Art behandelt. Vor allem Andy Warhol beschäftigte sich mit dem Prinzip der Serialität und führte in seiner Arbeit die technische und mediale Reproduzierbarkeit sowie deren spezifische Mythen und Stoffe vor. Suppendosen und Cola-Flaschen sind seine als Massenprodukte gezeigten Massenprodukte, und Maos Kopf wird bei ihm durch Repetition zum Tapetenmuster. Meist bleibt das Studium der Serialität bei Warhol freilich auf zweidimensionale Arbeiten beschränkt. Eine Ausnahme bilden die berühmten "Brillo-Boxes" von 1964 sowie andere – von Warhol jedoch jeweils eigens nachgebildete – Verpackungskartons, die allerdings kaum einmal höher als in vier oder fünf Lagen gestapelt wurden. Methoden der Warenpräsentation sind hier zwar adaptiert und als solche kenntlich gemacht, doch unterbleibt eine konsequente Erprobung der Möglichkeiten von Serialität im Bereich der Skulptur und des öffentlichen Raums.

Kastenhaus 424.8, 1996/97
Schwarzach, Moosbacher Anstalten

Erst in den letzten Jahren haben neben Wolfgang Winter und Berthold Hörbelt noch andere Künstler damit begonnen, diese Lücke zu schließen. So machte Katharina Fritsch Ende der achtziger Jahre die seriellen Arrangements von Waren in einigen ihrer Arbeiten zum Thema und brachte Wühltische oder Warengestelle in den Kontext von Kunst. Am bekanntesten wurde dabei ein Gestell mit 288 in neun Lagen aufgetürmten und gelb bemalten Madonnenfiguren ("Warengestell mit Madonnen", 1987/89).

Stephan Huber interessiert hingegen eher die Verfremdung, die etwas durch Repetition erfahren kann. Mit Vorliebe stellt er aufgeklappte Werkzeugkästen zu

that is normally displayed as a single commodity and thus perceived quite differently.

Winter/Hörbelt are less concerned with alienation that with an intelligent extension of something that can already be found in a beverage warehouse. On the one hand, this underscores the ready-made character of the beverage-case structures, since the artists not only use the cases themselves but also appropriate their customary mode of display for the most part as well. Yet they depart abruptly from the principle of the ready-made by assigning them a function that has little to do with merchandising aesthetics or warehouse logistics. The beverage-case structures actually create various kinds of useful space. They are less large-scale sculptures of the kind which must be viewed from a distance than contemporary and innovatively appropriate examples of festive and festival architecture. They have a gay and somewhat light-hearted, playful look, and they retain their charm as creations that might well have originated in a party mood even in the eighth or tenth variation.

The light effects that unfold inside the structures are surprisingly diverse and intense, while the towering stacks of so many cases lend the exterior an opulent quality. People become curious, and the occasional viewer may even venture to guess that someone is trying to get into the Guinness Book of Records or meeting the requirements of a daring bet. In short, Winter's and Hörbelt's beverage-case structures are genuine attractions—appealing sights in public areas, which they also represent in a subtle way as communal space. The cases gathered at these sites have already circulated through many households; they are taken out on deposit, returned when empty and exchanged for full ones. Thus they are a kind of modern relay baton that joins people together on the basis of a fundamental human need.

In this way, each of the beverage-case houses brings together for a short time something that is ordinarily distributed among many pantries, basements and kitchen cupboards. Similarly, people gather toget-

Stellprobe für Skulptur. Projekte in Münster, 1997

Säulen oder ganzen Wänden zusammen, und die Muster, die sich daraus ergeben, machen es schwer, das Grundmodul noch in seiner Funktionalität zu erkennen. Im Unterschied zu den Kastenhäusern ist hier nämlich ein seriell produzierter Gegenstand gestapelt, der als Ware sonst eher einzeln dargeboten und damit üblicherweise auch anders wahrgenommen wird.

Bei Winter/Hörbelt geht es freilich weniger um Verfremdung als um eine intelligente Weiterführung dessen, was bereits in einem Getränkelager zu finden ist. Damit wird der Readymade-Charakter der Kastenhäuser einerseits auf die Spitze getrieben, da neben den Kästen selbst auch ihre handelsübliche Anordnung weitgehend übernommen ist; indem dieser Anordnung jedoch auf einmal eine Funktion jenseits von Warenästhetik und Lagerlogistik zukommt, wird das Prinzip des Readymades andererseits auch gebrochen. Die Kastenhäuser schaffen tatsächlich vielfältig nutzbaren Raum, sie sind weniger Großskulpturen, die nach Betrachtung aus Distanz verlangen, als vielmehr zeitgenössische und neuartigadäquate Beispiele einer Fest- und Festivalarchitektur: Heiter und ein wenig verspielt wirken sie, und der Charme von etwas, das in Partylaune entstanden sein könnte, ist ihnen auch in der achten oder zehnten Variation noch nicht abhanden gekommen.

Die Lichteffekte, die sich im Inneren der Häuser ergeben, sind überraschend in ihrer Bandbreite und Intensität; von außen hingegen besitzt die Auftürmung so vieler Kästen Opulenz. Man wird neugierig, und mancher vermutet vielleicht, da wolle jemand ins Guiness-Buch der Rekorde gelangen oder eine tollkühne Wette einlösen. Die Kastenhäuser von Winter/Hörbelt sind also Attraktionen – Anziehungsorte im öffentlichen Raum, den sie als Gemeinschaftsraum überdies subtil repräsentieren. Die Kästen, die hier jeweils versammelt werden, zirkulierten bereits durch viele Haushalte, sie werden gegen Pfand ausgeliehen, leer wieder zurückgegeben und gegen andere ausgetauscht. So sind sie gleichsam Staffelhölzer der modernen Welt und verbinden die Menschen in einem ihrer elementaren Bedürfnisse.

In jedem aus Wasserkästen gebauten Haus wird also für kurze Zeit zusammengebracht, was sich sonst über viele Speisekammern, Keller und Küchen verteilt. Ähnlich treffen sich die Menschen im öffentlichen Raum und werden moment-

her in public space and form temporary communities whenever they emerge as individuals from their apartments and houses on special occasions. And in much the same sense that public space in our time is almost exclusively a place for special occasions and events, having lost many of its original everyday functions, the beverage case, one of the most mundane of everyday objects, suddenly makes its appearance in an unfamiliar guise. After the festive occasion, when the community begins to break apart again, the beverage-case structures are dismantled as well; the individual cases are returned to the distribution system and soon find themselves reindividualised and refilled in many different households.

Wolfgang Winter and Berthold Hörbelt make use of an element of modern infrastructure to achieve a contemporary interpretation of public space and, in doing so, to make the transitory, unfamiliar appearance it has in our world today visible to all. Beverage-case structures thus become a symbol for an era dominated by business and technology that is already influenced by mass-produced products more than by anything else. Without the potential offered by serial production, the successes of the great inventions of our century would have been inconceivable. Yet the manner in which contemporary people perceive the world, indeed the way in which they experience a sense of familiarity or home, is conditioned by the fact that nearly every object used in everyday life is a mass-produced product. As a rule, people reach for the same products over and over again and tend to find even a change in packaging design irritating. We are often helpless when shopping in foreign countries, as nothing on the shelves matches the product designs we are familiar with. We have grown used to DIN sizes and standardised dimensions in practically everything—from electrical plugs to printer paper and even beverage cases. There are very few things left in which deviations from these standards would not strike us as handicaps. Complete conformity with standard dimensions in products manufactured in large quantities can only be guaranteed by serial, technical methods of production, however.

The festive occasions and events that take place in and around the beverage-case structures have been so successful because the structures do not create a world in stark contrast to that of everyday life but instead adopt a piece of the everyday world and transform it into something very special. Discovering the

haft zu einer Gemeinschaft, wenn sie zu außergewöhnlichen Anlässen einzeln aus ihren Wohnungen und Häusern kommen. Und wie der öffentliche Raum heutzutage fast nur noch ein Ort für besondere Ereignisse ist und im Alltag viele seiner ursprünglichen Funktionen eingebüßt hat, erscheint nun auch mit dem Wasserkasten einer der alltäglichsten Gegenstände auf einmal in ungewohnter Manier, ja wird, auf einem Platz in beeindruckendem Plural gestapelt, getürmt und gereiht, selbst zu einem Ereignis. Nach dem Fest, wenn sich die Gemeinschaft wieder auflöst, werden auch die Kastenhäuser abgebaut, die einzelnen Wasserkästen gelangen in das Vertriebssystem zurück und finden sich bald wieder vereinzelt und neu gefüllt in verschiedenen Haushalten.

Wolfgang Winter und Berthold Hörbelt nutzen somit ein Stück moderner Infrastruktur, um den öffentlichen Raum zeitgemäß zu interpretieren und um dabei zugleich dessen in der heutigen Welt flüchtig-unalltägliche Erscheinung sichtbar zu machen. So werden die Kastenhäuser zu einem Sinnbild für eine von Technik und Wirtschaft geprägte Zeit, die ohnehin durch kaum etwas anderes mehr beeinflußt ist als durch Massenprodukte. Ohne die Möglichkeiten serieller Produktion ließen sich die Erfolge der großen Erfindungen des Jahrhunderts nicht vorstellen. Doch auch die Welterfahrung des heutigen Menschen, ja seine Art, Vertrautheit oder gar Heimat zu empfinden, ergibt sich daraus, daß fast alle Gegenstände des täglichen Lebens Massenprodukte sind. Man greift im Regal immer wieder nach denselben Produkten und ist bereits irritiert, wenn sich auch nur das Design der Verpackung verändert hat; im Ausland steht man entsprechend ratlos vor dem Regal, weil kaum etwas in die bekannten Produktmuster paßt. Ferner ist man an DIN-Größen und normierte Maße gewöhnt, egal ob es sich um Elektrostecker, Drucker-

Kastenhaus 1128.8/639.9 (Bauzaun), 1997
Münster, Salzstraße, Skulptur. Projekte in Munster

non-mundane in the everyday environment and making it visible to others is an art in itself. Even more importantly, however, it is the only way to create symbols capable of outlasting a single, passing event, symbols that have the power to promote an appreciation of the specific worlds they represent._

Sitzpolster, 1997

papier oder eben um Wasserkästen handelt. Es gibt nicht mehr viele Dinge, bei denen ein Abweichen von einer solchen Norm nicht als Handicap erscheint. Garantiert werden kann die Einhaltung von Standardmaßen bei zugleich großer Stückzahl jedoch nur durch seriell-technische Produktion.

Die Feste und Ereignisse, die sich in den Kastenhäusern und um sie herum abspielen, sind deshalb so gelungen, weil sie nicht eine strikte Gegenwelt zum Alltag der Menschen aufbauen, sondern ein Stück daraus als Material für etwas Besonderes verwenden und verwandeln. Es ist eine Kunst, das Unalltägliche im Alltäglichen zu entdecken und auch anderen sichtbar zu machen; vor allem aber ergeben sich auch nur daraus Sinnbilder, die eine einmalige Aktion überdauern und die das Verständnis der jeweiligen Welt, für die sie stehen, zu fördern vermögen.

Stellprobe für Skulptur. Projekte in Münster, 1997

Kastenhaus 740.10, 1997, Münster, Schloßplatz, Skulptur. Projekte in Münster

oben o.T., 1998, Wachskreide und Collage auf Papier, 59 x 80 cm

rechts Kastenhaus 1128.8/639.9 (Bauzaun, Innenansicht), 1997, Münster, Salzstraße, Skulptur. Projekte in Münster

folgende Seiten Kastenhaus 576.9, 1998, Salzburg, Alter Markt

Barbara Engelbach **TRANSITORY ARCHITECTURE AND OTHER SCULPTURES: Beverage-Case Buildings for the »Skulptur. Projects in Münster 1997«**

For three full months the kiosks erected by the artists Wolfgang Winter and Berthold Hörbelt served as welcoming centres for the Münster exhibition "Sculpture. Projects 1997" and as eye-catching attractions for visitors and residents of the city at the same time. With their functional orientation, they embodied one of the exhibition's central themes—art as public service, an astonishing contrast to the remainder of their oeuvre, in which we find both figural sculptures and large-scale spatial installations.

Wolfgang Winter and Berthold Hörbelt erected their beverage-case structures at selected prominent points in the city: the appealing surroundings of the Aasee, the striking façade of the castle and central spots such as the pedestrian zone on Salzstraße between the Church of St. Dominic and the Karstadt department store and the entrance lobby of the central railway station. At these places, passers-by and visitors to "Sculpture. Projects 1997" had the opportunity to obtain information about individual works and daily scheduled events or to buy catalogues and guides. In this way, the beverage-case structures functioned as information centres and kiosks.

The artists also assigned a specific function to their very first beverage-case building. Winter and Hörbelt were commissioned in 1996 to build a facility for recreation and retreat for patients in the garden of a rehabilitation centre in the town of Schwarzach. The pavilion they erected was designed in such a way that visitors could enter through a small opening into a circular room furnished with a carpet of moulded acrylic resin and places to sit. Clay reliefs completed by the patients decorate the beverage-case walls.

Much like this beverage-case building, the information centres in Münster appeared at first glance to have a great deal in common by virtue of their service character with a number of other works done for "Sculpture. Projects 1997", in which less emphasis was placed upon sculptural qualities in favour of greater concentration upon situation-specific and event-related aspects.

Barbara Engelbach **FLIEGENDE BAUTEN UND ANDERE SKULPTUREN**
Die Kastenhäuser während der »Skulptur. Projekte in Münster 1997«

Drei Monate lang waren die Informationshäuser der Künstler Wolfgang Winter und
Berthold Hörbelt Anlaufstellen der "Skulptur. Projekte 1997" und zugleich Blick-
fang für Besucher und Bewohner der Stadt. Mit ihrer Funktionsbezogenheit stan-
den sie für ein zentrales Thema der Ausstellung: Kunst als Dienstleistung.
Dagegen überrascht der Blick auf das sonstige Werk von Winter und Hörbelt, in
dem figurative Skulpturen gleichermaßen zu finden sind wie große Rauminstallationen.

Wolfgang Winter und Berthold Hörbelt hatten sich prominente Orte in der Stadt
ausgewählt, um ihre Kastenhäuser zu plazieren: die ansprechende Umgebung des
Aasees, die markante Fassade des Schlosses und zentrale Orte wie die Fußgängerzone in der Salzstraße zwischen Dominikanerkirche und Karstadt bzw. die
Eingangshalle des Bahnhofes. Passanten und Besucher der "Skulptur. Projekte

Atelier Frankfurt, 1996

The structures erected by Winter/ Hörbelt were quite restrained, however. They adapted to their surroundings by incorporating and reflecting upon elements of site architecture. The round buildings at the Aasee and inside the railway station looked like kiosks, while the curved shape of the pavilion in front of the baroque castle was planned as a kind of central architecture built on the basis of a trefoil arch. The beverage-case structure on Salzstraße also responded to its surroundings, as it closed off the square that opens up immediately outside the Karstadt department store opposite the Church of St. Dominic and incorporated with its elongated side wings the isolated flag poles of the art-and-construction project located at the same spot. Moreover, the functions of each individual structure were chosen with an eye to the specific characteristics of each location. The beverage-case structure in the pedestrian zone formed a passage following the direction of the street, the pavilion in front of the castle, with its bench and carpeting, invited visitors to stop and spend some time there, and the stand at the railway station offered waiting travellers a place to sit.

The beverage-case structures are by no means the kind of discreet art project in which the work of art is subdued to the extent that it does not even appear to be a work of art, however. Indeed, their unusual material causes them to stand out distinctly from their surroundings. Several thousand beverage cases from the "Genossenschaft Deutscher Brunnen eG" were used in the construction of the four structures. The cases were fitted with floor and ceiling sections connected with threaded rods. The precise names for these stable constructions were derived from the total number of cases they comprised and the number of cases stacked in a vertical segment. Thus Kastenhaus 710.10 consisted of 710 elements stacked in columns of ten cases each.

The temporary structures might never have

Atelier Frankfurt, 1995

1997" hatten dort die Möglichkeit, sich über einzelne Arbeiten und tägliche Veranstaltungen zu informieren, Kataloge und Kurzführer zu kaufen. Die Kastenhäuser fungierten somit als Informationsstand und Kiosk.

Auch ihrem ersten Kastenhaus hatten die Künstler eine Funktion zugewiesen: Winter/Hörbelt hatten 1996 den Auftrag erhalten, für den Garten eines Rehabilitationszentrums in Schwarzach einen Rückzugsort für die dort lebenden Patienten zu bauen. Der Pavillon ist so entworfen, daß man durch eine schmale Öffnung einen runden Raum betritt, der mit einem in Harz gegossenen Teppich und mit Sitzmöglichkeiten ausgestattet ist. Tonreliefs, die von den Patienten ergänzt werden, schmücken die Kastenwände. Wie dieses Kastenhaus hatten auch die Infohäuser in Münster auf den ersten Blick mit ihrem Dienstleistungsangebot viel gemeinsam mit einer Reihe von weiteren Arbeiten der "Skulptur. Projekte 1997", die weniger auf den skulpturalen, denn auf den situativen, ereignishaften Aspekt setzten.

Die Bauten von Winter/Hörbelt übten sich jedoch in Zurückhaltung. Sie fügten sich in ihre Umgebung ein, indem sie architektonische Elemente der Orte aufgriffen und kommentierten. Die Rundbauten am Aasee und im Bahnhof sahen wie Kioske aus, die geschwungene Form des Pavillons vor dem barocken Schloß war als eine auf einem Dreipaß aufgebaute Zentralarchitektur geplant. Auch das Kastenhaus auf der Salzstraße bezog sich auf den Umraum, weil es den unvermittelt sich öffnenden Platz vor Karstadt zur Dominikanerkirche hin abschloß und mit seinem langgestreckten Seitenflügel die vereinzelten Fahnenstangen des dortigen Kunst-am-Bau-Beitrages einband. Darüber hinaus waren die unterschiedlichen Funktionen auf die jeweiligen Orte abgestimmt. So war das Kastenhaus auf der Fußgängerzone eine Passage, die die Laufrichtung der Straße aufnahm, der Pavillon vor dem Schloß lud hingegen mit Bank und Teppichboden zum Verweilen auf, während der Stand am Bahnhof den Wartenden eine Sitzmöglichkeit bot.

Von einem diskreten künstlerischen Projekt, bei dem das Kunstwerk sich so zurücknimmt, daß es als solches nicht in Erscheinung tritt, kann bei den Kastenhäusern allerdings nicht gesprochen werden, denn zu deutlich heben sie sich durch ihr ungewöhnliches Baumaterial von der Umgebung ab. Mehrere tausend Getränkekästen von der "Genossenschaft Deutscher Brunnen eG" waren in

attracted notice, if it hadn't been for the reactions of irritation and amusement triggered in many visitors by the everyday character of their material. Exempted from the customary deposit fee and made available for "Sculpture. Projects 1997", the beverage cases could just as easily be found as banal utilitarian objects in practically anyone's basement storage area. Equally ordinary was the situation in which the first beverage-case structure originated. Having noticed empty beverage cases stacked in their studio, Winter and Hörbelt wondered whether they might be used for the framework of the garden house in Schwarzach.

Everyday objects have been regarded as "artworthy" ever since the early years of this century, when the Dadaists began to incorporate randomly discovered objects into their collages and Marcel Duchamp first exhibited mass-produced industrial goods as works of art. Although Duchamp revolutionised the concept of art with his ready-mades, art as an institution has long since appropriated this questioning attitude towards art for its own purposes. Today's artists can transplant found objects along with their fully intact original context into new spatial situations and rely nonetheless on the fact that their creative interventions in traditional exhibition space will be understood by all.

Unlike such objects, the neutral-looking, brown, green and orange beverage cases in the beverage-case structures erected by Winter and Hörbelt play a subordinate role vis-à-vis the overall design of the buildings. The artists assign the found object an entirely new function when they transform a beverage case into a building block or a stool. That they are really not intent upon achieving the alienating effect of the object torn from its normal context becomes evident in their works from the Same-Same series. Winter and Hörbelt have been experimenting since 1993 with a variety of found objects such as bottles, dolls or a Madonna figure from the fifties, which they reproduce using a casting process. They took a silicone film from the Madonna figure (which originally stood in a Frankfurt monastery chapel). Because the soft film stretches if it is not supported by a plaster mould, which means that the material seeks its own shape, so to speak, the products appear as variations on a basic form. Thus Winter and Hörbelt do not produce copies with their reproduction technique but instead create new sculptures with varying material and surface structures.

den vier Häusern verbaut. Durch Gewindestangen waren die Kästen mit Boden- und Deckenplatten verspannt. Die stabilen Konstruktionen erhielten ihre genaue Bezeichnung jeweils aus der Gesamtzahl der verwendeten Kästen und ihrer Anzahl in der Vertikalen. So bestand das "Kastenhaus 710.10" aus 710 Elementen, die zu einer Höhe von 10 Kästen übereinandergestapelt waren.

Die temporären Bauten wären womöglich nicht aufgefallen, hätte die Alltäglichkeit des Materials nicht viele Besucher erregt oder amüsiert. Die Kästen, die von der Ausleihgebühr befreit für die "Skulptur. Projekte 1997" zur Verfügung gestellt wurden, können heute als banaler Gebrauchsgegenstand in jedem Vorratskeller stehen. Ebenso alltäglich war die Situation, aus der das erste Kastenhaus hervorging: Im Atelier waren leere Getränkekästen übereinandergestapelt, als Winter/Hörbelt sich überlegten, ob sie nicht als Gerüst für das Schwarzach-Gartenhaus dienen könnten.

Nun sind Alltagsobjekte kunstwürdig, seit die Dadaisten Anfang des Jahrhunderts Zufallsfunde

Madonnen, 1996, Harz, variable Maße, Weil am Rhein, Kunstverein

Like the Madonna metamorphoses, Winter and Hörbelt regard their beverage-case structures as sculptures. Their exteriors are dominated by curved forms that appear compact and complete in themselves. Viewed from within, they communicate a new sense of space, for the sunlight that floods through the walls immerses the rooms in warm colours. Attention is focused upon the skeletal form of the cases and the interplay of light and shadows. Hermetically sealed on the outside, the shapes seem strikingly light and transparent on the inside. It was precisely this experience of space that Winter and Hörbelt described in remarks about their work on the first beverage-case structure: "By pure coincidence, the sun just happened to be shining into the studio on that particular day. The walls formed by the flesh-coloured cases became translucent in the sunlight, awakening the memory of the experience of shining a flashlight through one's hand in the dark and looking down at the transparent, shimmering, reddish flesh."

The model for Kastenhaus 710.10 basically reveals this same light-space, but without the shell. The artists carved the corresponding form from a clay block using pieces of wood, placed the small figures seen in the model inside and filled the hollow space with acrylic resin. The ridges and clay residues on the positive form serves as reminders of the production process. Thus the finished model not only shows the beverage-case building in reduced scale, it also conveys a comparable impression of its interior, since it looks like a rough glass building block, the compact material of which loses all traces of heaviness by virtue of its transparency.

We find attempts to come to grips with the subject of spatial boundaries and their dissolution in many of the works of Winter and Hörbelt. One such piece is Scobalit Raum, a piece completed in 1997. Using a material called Scobalit, which resembles translucent corrugated cardboard, Winter and Hörbelt erected curving walls in a gallery room. The closely aligned, milky walls gave structure to the surrounding space without creating the impression of confinement, since daylight still shined into the room.

Because light and transparency are important aspects of so many of the works of Winter and Hörbelt, we are quite naturally reminded when viewing the beverage-case houses of the glass house built by the architect Bruno Taut as an

in ihren Collagen verarbeiteten und Marcel Duchamp industriell gefertigte Massenprodukte als Kunstwerke ausstellte. Duchamp revolutionierte mit seinen Readymades den Kunstbegriff, jedoch ist diese Infragestellung der Kunst längst von der Institution Kunst vereinnahmt worden. Künstler können heute den gefundenen Gegenstand samt seines intakt belassenen Kontextes in eine neue räumliche Situation verpflanzen und doch darauf setzen, daß der künstlerische Eingriff in den traditionellen Ausstellungsraum verstanden wird.

Dagegen sind die neutral erscheinenden, braunen, grünen und orangenen Getränkekästen bei den Kastenhäusern von Winter/Hörbelt der Form des Gebäudes untergeordnet. Die Künstler weisen dem vorgefundenen Objekt eine neue Funktion zu, wenn sie den Getränkekasten in einen Baustein oder in einen Hocker verwandeln. Daß sie weniger den verfremdenden Effekt des aus seinem Kontext gerissenen Gegenstandes beabsichtigen, machen auch ihre Arbeiten aus der Serie ”Same Same” deutlich. Winter/Hörbelt experimentieren seit 1993 mit vorgefundenen Gegenständen wie Flaschen, Puppen oder einer bronzenen Madonnenfigur aus den fünfziger Jahren, die sie im Gußverfahren vervielfältigen. Von der Madonnenfigur, die aus einer Frankfurter Ordenskirche stammt, nahmen sie eine Silikonhaut ab. Weil die weiche Haut ohne stützende Gipshülle dem schweren Gußmaterial nachgibt, das Material sich also gleichsam selbst die Form sucht, erscheinen die Gebilde als Variationen einer Grundform. Mit dem Reproduktionsverfahren stellen Winter/ Hörbelt also keine Kopien des Originals her, vielmehr schaffen sie neue, in Material und Oberflächenstruktur veränderte Skulpturen.

Wie die Madonnenmetamorphosen verstehen Winter/Hörbelt auch die Kastenhäuser als Skulpturen. Von außen dominierten die geschwungenen Formen, die kompakt und geschlossen wirken. Innen vermittelte sich ein anderes Raumerlebnis, denn das einfallende Sonnenlicht tauchte die Räume in warme Farben. Die Aufmerksamkeit wurde auf die Skelettform der Kästen und auf das Licht- und Schattenspiel gelenkt. Die von außen hermetischen Formen wirkten von innen licht und transparent. Eben dieses Raumerlebnis beschreiben Winter/Hörbelt bei der Arbeit zu ihrem ersten Kastenhaus: "Zufällig schien gerade an diesem Tag die Sonne ins Atelier. Die Mauern aus den fleischfarbenen Kästen wurden bei Sonnen-

advertisement for the glass industry at the exhibition of the Deutscher Werkbund in Cologne in 1914. A dome made of coloured glass rose above the base of glass building blocks that rested upon a curved concrete pedestal. The coloured light shined through the dome into the transparent staircase area. Bruno Taut's glass house has its place within the tradition of the great exhibition halls that were designed to display goods from all over the world in the most effective manner possible. Its advertising function aside, Taut wanted the pavilion to demonstrate the technical potential inherent in this relatively new building material. The use of iron girders made it possible during the 19th century to enlarge building window surfaces, even to the point at which wall spaces in their iron constructions were filled with nothing but glass. Walls had abandoned their function as closing elements; interior and exterior mingled together. Experiments with iron and later steel construction figured most prominently in the structures that emerged with the growth of industrialisation – buildings such as railway stations, market halls and exhibition centres. One may see this kind of transparent construction, in which interior and exterior space interact, in the entrance lobby of the Münster railway station built during the fifties.

Aside from concern with the themes of transparency and light, we recognise another link between the beverage-case buildings and the glass palaces of the 19th century. Both are temporary architectures, for even the exhibition halls of the

Lappen, 1994
HOEWI 301, 150 x 60 x 10 cm

licht durchscheinend, weckten die Erinnerung an das Erlebnis, sich im Dunklen die Taschenlampe unter die Hand zu halten und von oben das transparent, rötlich schimmernde Fleisch zu betrachten."

Das Modell zum "Kastenhaus 710.10" zeigt im Grunde diesen Lichtraum, dem nur die Hülle fehlt. Die Künstler nahmen mit Holzscheiten die entsprechende Form aus einem Tonquader heraus, setzten die kleinen Figuren hinein, die im Modell zu sehen sind, und gossen den Hohlraum mit Kunstharz aus. Die Grate und Tonreste an der Positivform verweisen noch auf diesen Produktionsprozeß. Damit zeigt das fertige Modell nicht nur das Kastenhaus in verkleinertem Maßstab, es vermittelt auch einen vergleichbaren Eindruck von seinem Inneren, weil es wie ein roher Glasbaustein erscheint, dessen kompaktes Material durch seine Transparenz alle Schwere verliert.

Die Thematisierung von Raumgrenzen und deren Auflösung durch transparente Materialien ist in vielen Arbeiten von Winter/Hörbelt zu finden, wie z.B. in dem "Scobalit-Raum" von 1997. Mit dem Material Scobalit, das wie durchscheinende Wellpappe aussieht, zogen Winter/Hörbelt geschwungene Wände in den Raum einer Galerie ein. Die dichtstehenden, milchigen Wände strukturierten den Raum, ohne ihn zu beengen, weil das Tageslicht einfallen konnte.

Da Licht und Transparenz in so vielen Arbeiten von Winter/Hörbelt eine Rolle spielen, liegt es nicht fern, bei den Kastenhäusern an das "Glashaus" des Architekten Bruno Taut zu denken, das dieser 1914 als Werbung für die Glasindustrie in der Deutschen Werkbund-Ausstellung in Köln baute. Eine Kuppel aus gefärbtem Glas erhob sich über einem Sockel aus Glasbausteinen, der auf einem geschwungenen Betonpodest ruhte. In das durchsichtige Treppenhaus im Sockelgeschoß fiel das farbige Licht aus der Kuppel. Bruno Tauts Glashaus steht in der Tradition großer Ausstellungshallen, die Waren aus aller Welt möglichst wirkungsvoll präsentieren sollten. Über Reklamezwecke hinaus wollte Taut mit dem Pavillon die ästhetischen und technischen Möglichkeiten dieses vergleichsweise neuen Baumaterials vorführen. Mit der Verwendung von Eisenträgern wurde es im 19. Jahrhundert möglich, die Fensterflächen von Gebäuden zu vergrößern, bis hin zu Hallen, deren Eisenkonstruktionen nur noch mit Glas gefüllt waren. Die Wände hatten ihre

*period had to be built as transient structures that could be erected and dismant-
led quickly. This became feasible as soon as industry began manufacturing large
quantities of individual glass and iron elements in serial production. Winter's and
Hörbelt's beverage-case buildings also consist of serially produced elements that
make it possible to erect and dismantle them very quickly. And both share the
aspect of functional orientation. Whereas the exhibition halls of the 19th century
served the purposes of merchandise presentation, the beverage-case structures
provided space for the exchange of information during "Sculpture. Projects 1997".*

*The beverage-case structures of Winter and Hörbelt also share an ironic com-
ponent with Bruno Taut's glass house. Taut decorated the glass house with a frie-
ze adorned with rhymed couplets by the poet Paul Scheerbart. Scheerbart's ver-
ses lent Taut's didactic objective of encouraging a renewal of cultural values by
opening closed architecture a humorous lightness: "Glück ohne Glas – /Wie dumm
ist das!/Ohne einen Glaspalast/Ist das Leben eine Last./Das Glas bringt uns die
neue Zeit; / Backsteinkultur tut uns nur leid" (Happiness without glass – /How little class!/Life is just ballast/Without a glass palace/Glass rings in the new
age/Bricks and stones are no longer the rage.) Irony in the beverage-case structures is a matter of detail. The banal everyday material, which is inherently temporary because of its role in the system of deposit and exchange, is converted
into a transitory form of architecture which can be erected anew at different locations with modified form and function. Thus Winter and Hörbelt have accomplished
the happy reconciliation of sculpture and architecture in the everyday world of con-
sumerism—through plastic.*

abschließende Funktion verloren, Außen und Innen vermischten sich. Gerade in Bauten, die mit der Industrialisierung aufkamen, wie z.B. Bahnhöfe, Markt- und Ausstellungshallen, wurde mit Eisen- und später Stahlbetonskelettkonstruktionen experimentiert. In der Eingangshalle des Münsterschen Bahnhofs aus den 50er Jahren mag man ein solches transparentes Bauen erkennen, bei dem sich Außen- und Innenraum durchdringen.

Neben der Thematisierung von Transparenz und Licht kann noch eine zweite Parallele der Kastenhäuser zu den Glaspalästen des 19. Jahrhunderts festgestellt werden. Beide sind temporäre Architekturen, denn auch die Ausstellungshallen mußten damals als fliegende Bauten innerhalb kurzer Zeit aufgebaut und demontiert werden. Dies war nur möglich, weil die Einzelteile aus Eisen und Glas erstmals seriell in großen Mengen hergestellt werden konnten. Winter/Hörbelts Kastenhäuser bestehen gleichfalls aus seriell hergestellten Bauteilen, die den schnellen Auf- und Abbau ermöglichen. Beiden gemeinsam ist ebenfalls der Aspekt der Zweckgebundenheit: Dienten die Ausstellungshallen im 19. Jahrhundert der Präsentation von Waren, so boten die Kastenhäuser während der "Skulptur. Projekte 1997" Raum für Informationen.

Mit Bruno Tauts Glashaus teilen die Kastenhäuser von Winter/Hörbelt darüber hinaus eine ironische Komponente. Taut schmückte das Glashaus mit einem Fries, das mit Knittelversen des Dichters Paul Scheerbart geschmückt war. Dem aufklärerischen Anspruch Tauts, mit der Öffnung von geschlossener Architektur auch kulturelle Grundlagen der Gesellschaft zu erneuern, wurde durch Scheerbarts Sprüche eine humorvolle Leichtigkeit verliehen: "Glück ohne Glas – /Wie dumm ist das!/Ohne einen Glaspalast/Ist das Leben eine Last./Das Glas bringt uns die neue Zeit;/Backsteinkultur tut uns nur leid." Bei den Kastenhäusern steckt die Ironie im Detail: Das banale Alltagsmaterial, dem das Temporäre immanent ist, weil es in ein System von Pfand und Tausch eingebunden ist, wird nun in eine zeitlich begrenzte Architektur überführt, die an wechselnden Orten mit wechselnder Form und Funktion wieder aufgerichtet werden kann. Damit gelingen Winter/Hörbelt die glückliche Versöhnung von Skulptur und Architektur im konsumistischen Alltag, mit Kunststoff.

SAMESAME: Prototyp (Puppe Roswitha), 1994

SAMESAME: Tischfußball – 22 Variationen über eine Figur, 1994, diverse Materialien, 43 x 110 x 220 cm

Blöcke, 1995/96, HOEWI 301, variable Maße, Bremen, Kunsthalle, Kunstpreis der Böttcherstraße in Bremen 1999

Loch #3 und Abflußrohr, 1997, Harz, Metall, Holz, variable Maße, Frankfurt, Galerie Voges + Deisen
Scobalitraum, 1997, Scobalit, diverse Materialien, 300 x 350 x 800 cm, Frankfurt, Galerie Voges + Deisen

Amnon Barzel **_FROM WATER CRATES TO LIGHT MACHINES_**
Notes About a House without Foundations

*A house done from "nothing", without foundations, in the central square of the
Baroque town Salzburg. Prefabricated "poor" polymer plastic units of water crates
are the only building elements of this Kastenhaus created by Wolfgang Winter and
Berthold Hörbelt as a meeting place in a public space, a meeting with others, a
meeting with the self. This architec-*
tonic sculpture, built of 567 water
bottle cases of the "Deutsche
Mineralbrunnen AG" beverage com-
pany (the translation of the amount
of crates into the cabbalist numeri-
cal system creates the Hebrew phra-
se: houses of boxes in the town-
square...) acts as a light machine:
The daylight penetrates through the
openings of the prefabricated gree-
nish water crates to be refracted in

Entwurfszeichnung (Kastenhaus 576.9, Salzburg), 1998
Wachskreide und Collage auf Papier, 59 x 80 cm

*the inner space into numerous light spots, like the brush-strokes in the paintings
of the Impressionists, the pioneers of "ragmentation" as a basic concept of
modernity. Thus, the "light-fragments" within the Kastenhaus of Winter and Hörbelt
are moving during the day with the change of the sun rays, like a sundial, like the
Meridiana effect in the Basilica of St. Petronius in Bologna, where a moving spot
of light is measuring (drawing) the time on the floor. The walls of the Kastenhaus,
with its common, repeating units of massive polymer plastics, can be conceived
as a "luminous syndrome", as in the walls of Gothic cathedrals, defined by the
Austrian theorist Hans Sedlmayr as sources of light: "Walls which generate, not
reflect, the light itself."*

At night, the Kastenhaus takes on another role; it does not stop acting but

Amnon Barzel **VON MINERALWASSERKISTEN ZU LICHTMASCHINEN**

Gedanken zu einem Haus ohne Fundament

Ein Haus aus dem "Nichts", ohne Fundament, auf dem Marktplatz der Barockstadt Salzburg. Vorgefertigte Teile von Mineralwasserkisten aus "billigem" (polymerem) Plastik sind die einzigen Bausteine dieses Kastenhauses von Wolfgang Winter und Berthold Hörbelt, gedacht als Begegnungsstätte an einem öffentlichen Ort, als Begegnung mit anderen, mit sich selbst. Die begehbare Plastik aus 567 Wasserkisten der "Deutschen Mineralbrunnen AG" (überträgt man die Anzahl der Kisten in das Zahlensystem der Kabbala, ergibt sich der hebräische Satz: Kastenhaus auf dem Marktplatz) fungiert als Lichtmaschine: Das Tageslicht dringt durch die Öffnungen der vorgefertigten grünlichen Kästen und erscheint im inneren Raum verzehnfacht in Form kleiner Lichtpunkte, wie die Farbtupfer impressionistischer Maler, den Wegbereitern der "Fragmentierung" als Grundsatz der Moderne. Die "Lichtfragmente" in Winter und Hörbelts Kastenhaus verändern sich im Lauf des Tages wie bei einer Sonnenuhr mit den einfallenden Sonnenstrahlen, ähnlich dem Meridianeffekt in der Basilika San Petronio in Bologna, wo die Zeit mittels eines sich bewegenden Lichtpunkts am Boden gemessen (angezeigt) wird. Die Wände des Kastenhauses mit seinen gewöhnlichen, immer gleichen Plastikteilen können als "Leuchtsyndrom" begriffen werden, wie bei den Wänden gotischer Kathedralen, die von den österreichischen Theoretiker Hans Sedlmayr als Lichtquellen definiert werden: "Wände, die das Licht an sich erzeugen, nicht zurückwerfen."

Nachts erfüllt das Kastenhaus eine andere Funktion, agiert weiter: Es verwandelt sich in eine Laterna Magica. Das künstliche Licht des inneren Raums fällt als feine Lichtexplosion auf den Marktplatz, wie durch ein Glasfenster, das ohne Kapelle dasteht.

Winter und Hörbelt haben ihre "Begegnungsstätte" den Achsen des Platzes angepaßt, seiner Form und dem Umfeld, in dem sie steht. Ihre Absicht war Integration, die vielgerühmte Gastfreundschaft der Einwohner Salzburgs stand auf dem Prüfstein.

metamorphoses into a laterna magica. The artificial light from its inner space is transmitted toward the market-place as a delicate explosion of light, like a vitrage which has lost its chapel.

Winter and Hörbelt planed their "meeting-place" according to the axes of the town square, to its shape and to the urban network in which it is placed. They proposed an integration, challenging the reputed hospitality of the citizens of Salzburg.

The "poor" provisory Kastenhaus in front of the decorated bourgeois heritage of the Baroque with its stability and its aura of marble angles and golden saints was seen as a provocation—to the collective security with respect to property values, to the superiority of an exuberant past over the ever-changing concepts of any present.

Frequently, artists are seen as "urban guerrilla", but here Winter and Hörbelt not only endanger the economy of tourism, but propose a shift from property to culture as an expression of that it is not what we have that counts, but what we are.

The Kastenhaus, with its visual acoustics (a term coined by Le Corbusier), in its environment of "ine" architecture frozen in the stream of time, indicates the strive for content in a society which deals mainly with the container (architecture).

In their projects in Salzburg, Berlin, Bonn and future ones in Venice and on Etna, Wolfgang Winter and Berthold Hörbelt are searching for a new light: physical, conceptual, social and political. Their art is about lumen, as it is about enlightenment. Their houses have no foundations, they are as provisory as their building elements, but they carry an urgent contemporary message in our era of displacement, a definition crucial to the closure of our century. People and their cultures are moving from south to north, from east to west, forced to leave their homes to become refugees and homeless within an affluent post-technological urban society. The Kastenhaus is a message of tolerance, of understanding the "other", a work of art as a meeting-place for everybody in a town-square, done from "nothing", immersed in natural light.

It may remind us of Giacometti's "City Squares" sculptures, about which the artist himself remarked: "Every moment of the day people come together and drift

Das "billige", provisorische Kastenhaus vor dem prunkvollen barocken Kulturerbe des Bürgertums, seiner Stabilität und der Wirkung seiner Marmorkanten und vergoldeten Heiligen wurde jedoch als Provokation aufgefaßt, als Bedrohung des kollektiven Eigentumswerts, der Überlegenheit einer prächtigen Vergangenheit über die sich ständig verändernden Konzepte ein jeder Gegenwart.

o.T., 1998, Wachskreide und Collage auf Papier, 59 x 80 cm

Künstler gelten oft als "städtische Guerilla", hier aber gefährdeten Winter und Hörbelt nicht nur den Wirtschaftsfaktor Tourismus, sondern machten sich außerdem daran, Eigentum durch Kultur zu ersetzen, als Ausdruck davon, daß nicht das zählt, was man hat, sondern das, was man ist.

Das Kastenhaus mit seiner visuellen Akustik – ein Ausdruck, den Le Corbusier geprägt hat – in seiner "schönen", in der Zeit erstarrten Umgebung sind ein Hinweis auf das Streben nach Inhalt in einer Kultur, die sich hauptsächlich mit der Hülle (Architektur) befaßt.

In ihren Projekten in Salzburg, Berlin und Bonn und weiteren geplanten in Venedig und auf dem Ätna suchen Wolfgang Winter und Berthold Hörbelt nach einem neuen Licht – physikalisch, konzeptionell, gesellschaftlich und politisch. Ihre Kunst beschäftigt sich mit Lumen, mit Aufklärung. Ihre Häuser haben kein Fundament, sie sind so provisorisch wie ihre Bausteine, aber sie enthalten eine wichtige, zeitgemäße Botschaft in unserem Zeitalter der Verdrängung, eine Definition, die das Ende unseres Jahrhunderts treffend charakterisiert: Völker und ihre Kulturen ziehen von Süden nach Norden, von Osten nach Westen, müssen ihre Heimat verlassen und in der wohlhabenden posttechnologischen Gesellschaft als Flüchtlinge und Heimatlose existieren. Das Kastenhaus ist ein Plädoyer für Toleranz, für Verständnis für "das Andere", ein Kunstwerk als Begegnungsstätte für alle, auf einem Marktplatz, aus Nichts gebaut, in natürliches Licht getaucht.

Es erinnert uns vielleicht an Giacomettis "City Squares" Plastiken, die der

Entwurfszeichnung (Skulptur. Projekte in Münster), 1997
Mischtechnik auf Papier, 60 x 84 cm

apart, and approach each other again to try to make contact anew. The unceasingly form and reform living compositions of incredible complexity. What I want to express in everything I do is the totality of this life."

Vito Acconci, so active with his Private Projects in Public Space from "Houses for the Body" to a realisation of a six-unit house as a moving truck in 1991—wrote that "the person who chooses to do public art might be considered a refugee (fleeing from the gallery and museum system)."

Winter and Hörbelt do not have to be anxious: Their message in the era of displacement, done in the language of light, simplicity and humour, brings to mind the saying by Hugues de Saint-Victor from the 11th century: "Perfect is the person for whom the whole world is like a land of exile."

Künstler wie folgt überschrieb: "Jeden Augenblick treffen sich Leute und gehen auseinander, kommen wieder zusammen und versuchen, erneut Kontakt aufzunehmen. Sie bilden unaufhörlich lebende Kompositionen von ungeheurer Komplexität. Es ist diese Totalität des Lebens, die ich in allem, was ich mache, ausdrücken möchte."

Vito Acconci mit seinen privaten Projekten in öffentlichen Räumen wie etwa seinen Häusern für den Körper oder dem Sechs-Einheiten-Haus auf einem fahrenden Lastwagen, schrieb einmal, daß "der Künstler, der sich öffentlicher Kunst widmet, als Flüchtling gelten kann (auf der Flucht vor dem Galerie- und Museumssystem)."

Winter und Hörbelt können beruhigt sein: Ihre Botschaft im Zeitalter der Verdrängung, in der Sprache des Lichts, der Einfachheit und des Humors, erinnert an ein Wort von Hugues de Saint-Victor aus dem elften Jahrhundert: "Perfekt ist der, der die ganze Welt als Exil begreift."

folgende Seiten Kastenhaus 560.10 (Doppler), 1999, Bremen, Kunsthalle
Kunstpreis der Böttcherstraße in Bremen 1999

LEBENSMITTEL
OBST UND GEMÜSE
FLEISCH
RISCH
MeLteM supermarkt
supermarkt
MELTEM
Rückertstraße
44-32
5

BIOGRAFIE / *BIOGRAPHY*

Wolfgang Winter

1960	born in Offenbach
1985–89	attended the Hochschule bildender Künste (HbK), Kassel
1987–89	attended the Städelschule, Frankfurt am Main
seit 1992	*Same-Same* projects in co-operation with Berthold Hörbelt

Berthold Hörbelt

1958	born in Coesfeld
1983–89	attended the Hochschule bildender Künste (HbK), Kassel
seit 1992	*Same-Same* projects in co-operation with Wolfgang Winter

The artists live and work in Havixbeck and Frankfurt am Main.

EINZELAUSSTELLUNGEN / GRUPPENAUSSTELLUNGEN (AUSWAHL)
SOLO EXHIBITIONS / GROUP EXHIBITIONS (SELECTION)

1999   Kastenhaus 248.8, Marburg

1998   Kastenhaus 443.10, Salzburg
Kastenhaus 1330.11, Museumsplatz Bonn
Kastenhaus 378.9, Soloshow art cologne
Kastenhaus 4/288.12 (Vier Solitäre)

1997   Galerie Edition Voges + Deisen, Frankfurt (K)

1996   ACP Galerie, Salzburg

1995   Galerie Edition Voges + Deisen, Frankfurt

1994   Galerie Tabea Langenkamp, Düsseldorf (K)

1993   "Same Same"; Produzentengalerie, Kassel

1999   Kunstpreis der Boettcherstraße in Bremen, Kunsthalle Bremen
48. Biennale di Venezia, Venice
Skulptur-Biennale im Münsterland 1999
Projeto Arte/Cidade, São Paulo

1998   Kastenhaus 2640.15, Cinema Projects, Künstlerhaus Bethanien, Berlin
ACP Galerie, Salzburg

1997   Skulptur.Projekte in Münster 1997 (K)

1996   Galerie Voges + Deisen zu Gast bei Galerie vierte etage, Berlin
Kunstverein Weil am Rhein

1995   Dem Herkules zu Füßen, Museum Fridericianum, Kassel (K)
C&L Deutsche Revision, Ausstattungsprogramm mit Lehrern und Schülern der Städelschule (K)

PROJEKTE IM ÖFFENTLICHEN RAUM
PROJECTS IN PUBLIC SPACE

1992   Katholische Hochschule St. Georgen, Frankfurt am Main
Renovation of the seminar church, interior design in co-operation with Prof. Ernst Studer and Ulrich Rückriem
Smokestack project, Frankfurt am Main

1996   Garden design and pavilion construction (*Kastenhaus 424.8*)
Garden of the senses for the rehabilitation centre Moosbacher Anstalten, Schwarzach

1998   Playground ring, Münster

PREISE UND STIPENDIEN
AWARDS AND GRANTS

1993   Kunstpreis der Stadt Baunatal
1996   Work grant from the Stiftung Leube, Salzburg

KATALOGE (AUSWAHL)
CATALOGUES (SELECTION)

Wolfgang Winter/Berthold Hörbelt, Galerie Tabea Langenkamp, Düsseldorf, 1994
Dem Herkules zu Füßen, Museum Fridericianum, Kassel, 1995
C&L, Deutsche Revision AG KUNST, Frankfurt, 1995
Skulptur. Projekte in Münster, Hrsg. Kasper König, Florian Matzner, Klaus Bußmann, Ostfildern, 1997

Wolfgang Winter/Berthold Hörbelt, Galerie Voges + Deisen, Frankfurt, 1997
Kunstpreis der Boettcherstraße in Bremen, Bremen, 1999

ARTIKEL (AUSWAHL)
PUBLISHED ARTICLES (SELECTION)

"100 Tage Kunst und Kultur im öffentlichem Raum", K + S – *Die Zeitung am Sonntag*, 6/22/97
"Kunstkratzer im Stadtbild", AD – *Architectural Digest*, August/September 1997, S./p. 122
"Magic Münster", *Bunte*, Heft 26, 1997, S./p. 62
"Münster tut gut", *art – Das Kunstmagazin*, August 1997, S./p. 44
"Skulptur. Projekte in Münster", *Kunstforum International*, Vol. 138, 1997, S./p. 361
"The Cinema Projekt", in *Kunstforum International*, Vol. 143, 1998
"Von der klassischen Moderne bis zu den Neuen Medien", *Frankfurter Rundschau*, 9/11/97
Michael Hierholzer, "Skulpturen aus Wasserkästen", *FAZ*, 9/28/97
Nicola Kühn, "Weg mit dem Ballast der Autonomie", *Der Tagesspiegel*, 7/6/97
Th. Fechner-Smarsly, "Sinnliche Promendade", *Frankfurter Rundschau*, 6/26/97
Wolfgang Welsch, "Aesthetisierung: Schrecken und Chance", *ZYMA – Art Today*, Nr. 2, 1996, S./p. 20

PHOTONACHWEIS
PHOTO CREDITS

David Brandt 42, 43, 45, 46, 47
Tim Esser 17, 24, 30, 31, 78, 90+91
Wolfgang Träger 34
Roman Mensing 2+3, 57, 61
Julia Ficht 4
Ghezzi 13, 64+65
Heinrich Hübner 14
Horst Ziegenfusz 75
Wolfgang Günzel 82, 83

DIE KÜNSTLER DANKEN
ACKNOWLEDGEMENTS

Genossenschaft Deutscher Brunnen/Herrn Wolff,
Herrn Dr. Rottke; Fa. Koch Ingenieure/
Ulrich Manthey; Fa. Delbrouck-Plastik; Fa. Leube/
Susanne + Susi Zrost; Peter Schuengel;
Christine Lanzenbacher, Heike Dander; Tim Esser;
Frank Rotfuß, Markus Lohmann, Philip Zaiser,
Monica und/and Catharina, Marie-Theres, Lea
und/and Sophia, unseren Eltern/our parents sowie
der/the Galerie Voges + Deisen/Frankfurt am Main
und den Autoren/and the authors sowie/and Elke
Neumann

Abbildungen/Illustrations
S. 2+3 Aufbau, 1997, Skulptur. Projekte in Münster
S. 4 Kastenhaus 576.9 (Innenansicht/interior view),
1998, Salzburg/Alter Markt
S. 6+7 Modell (Passage), 1998
Einmachgläser, Gips, Knetfiguren/canning jars, plaster,
clay figures, ca./approx. 30 x 40 x 180 cm
S. 11 Kastenhaus 4/288.12 (Vier Solitäre), 1998
Munich, Marienhof
S. 92 Melem, 1999, Frankfurt/Hanauer Landstraße

IMPRESSUM / *COLOPHON*

Herausgegeben von/Edited by
Florian Matzner

Übersetzungen/Translations
Claudia Spinner (Text A. Barzel)
John S. Southard (Text F. Matzner, Text W. Ullrich,
        Text B. Engelbach, appendix/Anhang)

Gestaltung/Design
Saskia H. Rothfischer

Reproduktionen/Reproductions
Fotosatz Weyhing, Ostfildern

Gesamtherstellung/Printed by
Dr. Cantz'sche Druckerei, Ostfildern

© 1999 Herausgeber/Editor, Künstler/artists,
Autoren/authors, und/and Hatje Cantz Publishers

Erschienen im/Published by
Hatje Cantz Publishers
Senefelderstraße 12
73760 Ostfildern-Ruit
T. 0711/44 05-0; F. 0711/44 05-220
Internet: www.hatjecantz.de

Distribution in the US
D.A.P., Distributed Art Publishers, Inc.
155 Avenue of the Americas, Second Floor
USA-New York, N.Y. 10013-1507
T. 0 01/2 12/6 27 19 99
F. 0 01/2 12/6 27 94 84

ISBN 3-7757-0843-X

Printed in Germany

BISHER ERSCHIENEN / ALREADY AVAILABLE

Marina Abramović
Biography

Stephan Balkenhol
Plätze/Orte/Situationen

Jonathan Borofsky
Dem Publikum gewidmet
Dedicated to the Audience

Hanne Darboven
Konstruiert, Literarisch, Musikalisch

Einszueins
Horst Antes, Joachim Sartorius

Eva & Adele
Nota – Licht auf Weimar

Jan Fabre im Gespräch mit Jan Hoet
und Hugo de Greef

FLATZ
Bodycheck – Physical Sculpture No. 5

FLATZ
Physical Sculptures

Johannes Geccelli
Texte aus dem Atelier

Glück
Ein Symposium

Karl Otto Götz im Gespräch

Antony Gormley
Total Strangers

Dan Graham
Interviews

Mary Heilmann
Farbe und Lust – Color and Passion

Stephan von Huene
Tischtänzer

Illusion und Simulation
Begegnung mit der Realität

Jörg Immendorff
The Rake's Progress

Kazuo Katase
Räume der Gegenwelt

Tadashi Kawamata
Field Work

On Kawara
June 9, 1991. From "Today" Series
(1955–...)

Mike Kelley im Gespräch

B
Gespräche mit Martin Kippenberger

Martin Kippenberger
The Last Stop West

Königsmacher?
Zur Kunstkritik heute

Joseph Kosuth
No Exit – Kein Ausweg

Mischa Kuball
Sprach Platz Sprache

Kunst im Abseits
Zwei Gespräche mit Catherine David

Wolfgang Laib
Eine Reise

Bertrand Lavier
Argo

Louise Lawler
For Sale

Thomas Lehnerer
Ethik ins Werk

Bernhard Leitner
Geometrie der Töne

Markus Lüpertz
Deutsche Motive

Matthew McCaslin
Ausstellung – Exhibitions

Allan McCollum/Laurie Simmons
Actual Photos

Maurizio Nannucci
Hortus Botanicus

Roman Opalka
Anti-Sisyphos

Original
Symposium Salzburger
Kunstverein

Haralampi Oroschakoff
Entwürfe. Eine Textsammlung
1980–1994

Der Ort der Bilder
Jay-Young Park im Gespräch

Heribert C. Ottersbach
Erinnerte Bilder

Nam June Paik
Baroque Laser

Christos Papoulias
Hypertopos

Partenheimer
Architektur und Skulptur

Sigmar Polke
Schleifenbilder

Positionen zur Kunst
Positions in Art

Fritz Rahmann
U.A. Zwei Rösser

Igor Sacharow-Ross
Feuer und Fest – Fire and Festival

Bernard Schultze
Pictor Poeta

Susanna Taras
Beiwerk

Günther Umberg
Raum für Malerei

Lois Weinberger
Texte

Lawrence Weiner, Ulrich Rückriem
öffentlich – public freehold

Ute Wrede
Mohn und Gedächtnis

Erwin Wurm
Expedition

Erwin Wurm
One minute sculptures

Johanes Zechner
Der Afrikanische Koffer

R E I H E   C A N T Z